Discovering Motherhood

Edited by
Heidi L. Brennan
Pamela M. Goresh
Catherine H. Myers

This book was written, edited, illustrated and published by mothers. It offers support and information
to women as they become mothers, as well as insight
into the lives of mothers who choose to be at home.

Published by
Mothers At Home™
8310-A Old Courthouse Road
Vienna, Virginia 22182

D1410085

Discovering Motherhood

Editorial Team

Executive Editors
Heidi L. Brennan
Pamela M. Goresh
Catherine H. Myers

Contributing Editors
Joanne Bruun
Mary Fisk Docksai
Lilli D. Hausenfluck
Cornelia Odom

Poetry Editor
Nedda Davis

Manuscript Reviewers
Gae Bomier
Barbara Kneeland
Mary Ellen McCormick
Diane Morse
Betsy Moyer

Editorial Assistants
Cari Bilyeu Clark
Elizabeth Foss
Laura Jones
Athena Williams

Artist and Illustrator
Susan Somerfield Stoffle

Production Team

Publication Director
Catherine H. Myers

Production Coordinator
Mary Fisk Docksai

Graphic Designer
Christina Davenport

Art Coordinator
Cathleen Gardner

Production Assistants
Alice Lee
Tammy DeMartino
Lee Miller

Typesetting
Mary Fisk Docksai
Pat Parkhurst Higgins

Special Acknowledgement

Thank you to these supporters and advisors, who reviewed this book in draft form and made valuable suggestions to us:

Glenn Austin, M.D.
Past President
American Academy of Pediatrics
Los Altos, California

Elliott Barker, M.D.
Founder
Canadian Society for the
Prevention of Cruelty to Children
Ontario, Canada

Deborah Fallows
Author, *A Mother's Work*
Washington, D.C.

Susan Robison, Ph.D.
Psychologist
Ellicott City, Maryland

Burton White, Ph.D.
Founder
Center For Parent Education
Newton, Massachusetts

Library Of Congress Cataloging-In-Publication Data:

Discovering Motherhood / edited by Heidi L. Brennan, Pamela M. Goresh, Catherine H. Myers : [artist and illustrator, Susan Somerfield Stoffle].
     p.   cm.
ISBN 0-9631188-0-3
1. Motherhood--United States. 2. Mothers--United States--Psychology. I. Brennan, Heidi L., 1953-
II. Goresh, Pamela M., 1953- . III. Myers, Catherine H., 1954-
HQ759.D57 1991
306.874'3--dc20

91-43333
CIP

Table Of Contents

A Note From The Editors

Discovering Motherhood grew out of the thoughts and feelings of thousands of mothers. The development of this extended community began in 1984, when three mothers founded our national nonprofit organization, **Mothers At Home.** Concerned by our society's misconceptions and stereotypes about mothers, they also had noted the lack of support for those who choose (or would like to choose) to be at home with their children. To support these mothers, they began publishing a monthly journal, **Welcome Home**. From the very first issue, mothers with diverse experiences and personal situations have responded with gratitude and enthusiasm. Every month, the pages of **Welcome Home** are filled with articles, poems, and art created and donated by these mothers.

Thousands of women write to us each year. They send letters, manuscripts, and responses to questions and surveys. They tell us how important it is to them to be part of our community, sharing information and understanding. We have spent many hours learning from these mothers, discussing our own experiences and observations as well. The insight we have gained has shown us that new mothers, faced with significant physical, emotional, and social changes, are especially in need of assistance while they make the transition into motherhood. This book emerged from our desire to help by providing information and support.

Discovering Motherhood gathers the voices of many mothers to convey the essence of a home-centered life. The articles we have collected affirm the critical importance of nurturing and note the subtle, daily interactions out of which trusting relationships are built. They explore the potential for personal growth to be realized through mothering.

This book was written, edited, illustrated, designed, and published by mothers. It took almost two years to complete—far longer than we first anticipated. Mothering has taught us to be patient, to respect the process as much as the product. It would not have been the same book had we been able to devote our full attention to it for a shorter period of time. Its slow development gave us the opportunity to reflect on many things: the range of information we wanted to include, the organization of the sections, the editing of the articles, the design. The pace of production work slowed periodically, as other commitments demanded our attention. After stepping back, we always returned with renewed energy and fresh insight. By taking time, we could gather opinions and discuss them, think about them, and then reach a consensus on most decisions.

Countless volunteer hours, in addition to the dedicated work of our staff, made this book possible. The shared commitment of many family members, including our husbands, our parents, and our children, enabled us to complete this project. We hope you will feel the spirit of camaraderie and friendship with which it was created. Each mother who contributed to this effort offers a glimpse into her life, and together we extend an invitation to you: join us in **Discovering Motherhood.** ♥

Redefining Ourselves

The Road Less Traveled

by Robin Morris

Two roads diverged in a wood and I — I took the one less traveled by, and that has made all the difference.

Robert Frost

I have been thinking about the road less traveled. Since I first heard those words they have been my ideal. It is not so much because I dislike the beaten path, nor that the unbeaten path holds some great lure. It is because I desperately want to have a life that, in the end at least, "made all the difference." A life as big and as grand as my personal potential would allow.

I did not realize the two roads would diverge at motherhood, although in retrospect it is the most natural place for this to happen to a woman. Yet diverge they did, and choices have been required.

So which is the road less traveled by? Certainly mothering at home is a trodden path if ever there was one. On the other hand, my generation – the ME generation – encouraged "having it all," and I am choosing a theme closer to giving it all.

I think of the old German proverb which asks, "What is the use of running if we are not on the right road?" Indeed, what is the use of choosing the prescribed road, be it greater or lesser traveled, if it takes you somewhere you really did not want to go? Today, I have chosen to be a mother at home. My idea of a big and grand life, not to mention my conception of my personal potential, have changed. Indeed, they have grown. And I no longer need another person – even as lovely a poet as Robert Frost – to point me in the direction of what will make all the difference. I instinctively know. Motherhood has given me that, and I will be eternally grateful.

How odd that in giving myself away, I have found myself at last. ♥

Transitions

by Heidi L. Brennan

Like many women expecting their first baby, I spent a lot of time making plans. I practiced with my husband for labor and delivery. I organized my baby's room and purchased clothing and supplies. I prepared for the loss of some of my employment income. I even planned to continue my career at home by leaving my job a few months before my due date in order to develop a possible home-based business.

What I simply could not plan for was my emotions. I wasn't able to adequately anticipate how I would **feel** about my new baby, as well as about myself and our new life as a family. As I left the hospital, I was overwhelmed by unfamiliar feelings of protectiveness and even fear. I did not want to let my new son out of my sight. At the same time, I did not know how I would possibly take care of him.

My planning, as useful as it had been, could not have addressed the emotional changes inside of me. Suddenly I needed others in unexpected ways. My mother came to stay for two weeks, and my husband worked shorter hours. This was a special time for us in which we began to explore our new roles as mother, father, and grandmother. Together, my husband and mother helped me to recover physically from childbirth. However, the emotional support that I received from them was as important to me as the physical care. As a new mother, I needed nurturing almost as much as did our baby.

All too soon, my mother's visit came to an end, and my husband returned to his usual schedule. Alone in my house with our new son, I found the silence deafening, broken only by his gurgles as he nursed for hours on end. I needed other people. I called friends, but phone conversations have to come to an end. I stared blankly at the phone when I wasn't using it. Who did I want to call, and what did I want to ask her?

While many of my questions were about baby care, others were about motherhood itself. One question, however, seemed to be following me around, one that I really couldn't ask aloud. "Who was I, now that I was a mother?"

While I knew that I was the same person, I also felt myself to be different. My bonds with my son had grown stronger, and I had begun to change my expectations about motherhood. Having a child had transformed me, and now I wasn't sure what my new life meant and how I was going to live it. I had become an adult in a culture that said, "Don't base your identity on motherhood." Yet how could I explain my intense desire to give my time to our baby? I felt that society was asking me to ignore my feelings and to believe that it was wrong to make childrearing the central focus of my life. I was not prepared for this internal conflict, and I felt alone as I struggled with it.

When I turned on the television, I was mocked by its images of contemporary women. The radio was no substitute for conversation or friendship. My husband's workdays seemed to last forever, and I longed for the weekends when he was home.

I lived far away from family and relatives. I knew only a few neighbors. Home alone, my adjustment to motherhood was a time of stress and confusion. It was not that I couldn't ever "get out." But trips to the market and walks in my neighborhood did not replace what I needed most – the frequent and spontaneous contact with people who knew me, cared about me, respected me, and included me in their daily activities. I had enjoyed this type of support at my former workplace, and I now missed it. This, then, was something else that I hadn't planned for – the loss of community – a place where a person shares common interests and purpose.

My relationship with my baby was just developing, and I missed the daily feedback that would have helped me to feel secure and competent in my new role. I knew what was expected of me in my previous job and now the old workplace begged for my return in both subtle and not-so-subtle ways.

The pull of my work community had begun long before my baby was born. People would say: "When will you return to work?" "We need you here." "What kind of child care are you looking for?" "You would be bored at home." Even after I was home, I continued to receive the same kinds of questions and comments.

It became apparent to me that my career had been, in many ways, my most important source of identity and friendship. I felt a real sense of loss when I separated myself from daily contact with people who had appreciated my work and reinforced my self-image. I understood how a new mother might long to return to her old job, even a mother who had planned to be at home.

I searched for an explanation for my confusion. I remembered a time, several years before, when I had accepted a new job in a different state. It was a wonderful opportunity, and I was very excited about it. But the pain of leaving so many familiar things, especially relationships where I felt valued, prevented me from enjoying my new job and developing friendships for at least six months. I had to adjust my skills to different responsibilities and to a changed work environment. It took time for me to prove to myself, as well as to the others, that I was capable in my new position.

I began to realize that my transition to at-home motherhood was mirroring that job experience. I could not avoid feeling sad at the loss of my work identity. As I started to accept that loss, I was able to get to know the "mother" within me.

While I felt the tug of my former job, I knew that even if I did return, things would not be the same. My life was different now. I needed the give-and-take of a community, but I didn't want one that would separate me from my child.

At first, I wanted companionship and support. I joined several local mothers' support groups, became actively involved in my neighborhood, and developed a growing network of friends with whom I could share my joys and concerns as a mother.

With time and effort, I began to find my mothering community. My new peers were people I liked and respected. I found role models who showed me how to include a variety of activities into my new life. I developed confidence in my nurturing abilities. Eventually, I learned interesting ways to use my former job skills both in the management of my home and in volunteer and civic work. As I began motherhood, I had been concerned that I would lose these skills. In reality, I found that they were enhanced by my motherwork.

My transition into motherhood was not accomplished in a few weeks or even a few months. It was at least two years before I felt "at-home" in my new role. Looking back at that period of time, I realize that I could not have planned for the changes which occurred inside of me. Nor could I have anticipated the surprises that having a child brought me. Motherhood is far more challenging and fulfilling than I had thought it would be. The effort I put into my mothering is rewarded in many different ways. Before I could make these discoveries, I had to accept the process of change: the confusion, the questions, and then newfound confidence and abilities.

As I began to understand the significance of my nurturing role, I gained a greater sense of purpose for my life. I find that opportunities for mental, emotional, and spiritual growth continue to unfold along this path of motherhood.♥ © 1991

*Heidi L. Brennan, who lives in Arlington, Virginia, is the mother of four children, ages seven months to seven years. She enjoys reading, dancing, golfing, and volunteer work. Heidi is Co-Director of **Mothers At Home,** the publishers of **Welcome Home.***

I'm Not The Person I Was

by Pam Svoboda

I had no doubt I would go back to work after my first baby was born. Throughout all nine months of pregnancy, I assured everyone that I was not a "homebody," that I'd be bored at home, and that I needed to be out in the world. I convinced my boss that I would come back to my job at the greenhouse. I had no reason to believe I wouldn't. After all, I loved it, finding great satisfaction in digging my hands in the soil and working with green plants. The baby would be born in March and I would be ready to get back to the vegetables and flowers in May. No problem.

Then she was born. I immediately fell deeply in love with this small, soft, warm baby. I had no idea she would be so special! As each day of her life passed, I did what seemed impossible. I grew to love her more. I loved everything about her: her clenched fist, her rosebud mouth, her smell, her cry – and my heart felt it would burst with her smile.

Still, I didn't think I could stand to be at home all the time. I felt cooped up after only a few weeks. Although I had my baby to look after, I felt lonely during the day when my husband was gone. I longed for some adult conversation. I was bored, and we missed the extra money. My husband made enough to pay the bills, but there wasn't much left over for anything else. So after just six short weeks I had a babysitter lined up, was squished into my old clothes, and was ready to get back to my job.

A funny thing happened, however. While I'd been home, I missed my job. Yet, now I missed my baby terribly! I constantly wondered what she was doing. Was she crying? Did she need me? Was she tasting her fingers or wiggling her toes? I started to be a "clock watcher." I couldn't wait for quitting time. On my breaks I'd rush to call my sitter.

"Hi, are you guys doing all right?"

"Yeah, we're fine. I've just finished feeding her and she's gone back to sleep."

"OK, just thought I'd call and check."

I was too embarrassed to ask the other questions on my mind. Did she blow milk bubbles at you? Has she fussed or smiled? Did she wrinkle up her brow and study her rattle? It didn't take me long to realize that what I really wanted was to be a fulltime twenty-four-hours-a-day mother. I know now that I had to go back to work to realize this. My heart was not in my job any more. At first I told myself I needed to give it more time, that I eventually would adjust, but the more time I spent away from my baby, the more I longed to be with her. Finally, after repeated debates with myself, I gave my two-week notice. I never have regretted the decision I made.

I stayed home with my daughter for two years until she was a little more independent before returning to work parttime at the greenhouse again. I worked about fifteen hours a week; a few evenings, and weekends when her father could be home with her. However, the job I loved best and the one I considered most important was my work at home.

Four months ago we were blessed with a beautiful baby boy who captured my heart just as quickly and as surely as my firstborn did. I knew from the moment I found out I was pregnant I would want to be with this baby, too. For me, the greenhouse is on hold again.

I do not feel at all that I am making a sacrifice. I *want* to be at home. I'm not the same person I was before I had children. I've learned so much about myself through them. I know I am no less of a person because at the present I don't have what some people call a "career." Of course, I grow restless at times, but I know this happens with any job.

Not too long ago, my daughter, then four years old, ran up to me and said, "Mommy, I love you more than I can." It brought tears to my eyes because that's exactly how I feel about her. My life as a mother at home is challenging, rewarding, and fulfilling. What's more, I'm enjoying it.♥
© 1986

Pam Svoboda is the mother of three children: Heather (ten), Seth (six), and Luke (two). She works about ten hours a week at a local college, heading up a program to teach adults reading, writing, and arithmetic. Her home is in McCook, Nebraska.

(My first) Mother's Day

From my lap
your eyes smile at me as we rock
time stands still.

the world out there whirls by
hurrying, meetings, schedules,
appointments, responsibilities, traffic.
I remember.

but we two
in this rain-drenched woods
share an eternal stillness
stolen from that hectic life.
we retreat to enjoy our secret
day after day.

moms and babies everywhere join us
in this precious fleeting joy.

I turned down another job
offer today.

Marcia Crosbie

What Do I Want Out Of Life?

by Susan M. Koshute

When I discovered I was pregnant, my emotions were in turmoil, ranging from elation to anxiety. Raising a family as a fulltime mother had been a lifelong dream. Thus, a dichotomy arose when I contemplated the option of being a working mother.

The decision whether to quit my job as administrative dietician at a 500-bed hospital was difficult and frustrating. After three years of being in a management position where I designed training programs and supervised food service employees, I only recently had become comfortable in my professional role and was reluctant to give it up.

Inner Struggle

My husband Mark was confused by my ambivalence. Before we were married, we had discussed childrearing, agreeing that when our first child was born I would quit my job. Suddenly, I was changing my mind.

We had many heated discussions regarding the choice between my career as a dietician and one of fulltime mothering. As prospective parents we were uncertain of demands and responsibilities. Though he preferred that I quit my job, Mark promised to support whatever decision I made.

It was not the loss of a paycheck that concerned me. My inner struggle stemmed from a growing fear of losing my self-esteem. Because we tend to define ourselves by our occupations, I was uncomfortable with my prospective self-image; motherhood was a role that I identified only with other women. Psychologically I had an unbalanced perspective on how my job, family, friends, and self were related. Once I had known the answer to "What do I want out of life?" but now I was puzzled.

I arranged a three months' leave of absence. Assuring the employees I would return, at least on a parttime basis, I delegated my duties to the very supervisors I had trained. Phillip was born on schedule, August 11, 1983, via an unexpected cesarean section. I faithfully kept to an exercise regimen of walking and isometrics, and within a month I had recuperated.

Weekly phone calls and occasional visits to the dietary department kept me in contact with my boss. We negotiated a compromise that accommodated my situation as a mother, yet helped save dollars on the staffing budget. We agreed I would work a maximum of ten hours a week. Mark agreed to take care of Phillip in the evenings and on weekends. I would hire a sitter during the day. My boss described the compromise as a "perfect fit." For me it represented the best of both worlds: I would have time for my child, and I would be keeping up to date in my field.

Unexpected Changes

Despite these well-thought-out plans, the unexpected happened. One week before my scheduled return to work, my car broke down irreparably. Recently having bought a home, we were unable to add a car payment to our list of monthly bills. Without any daytime transportation, I had no choice but to write my letter of resignation.

At first I was so busy organizing the contents of our new home, I did not have the time to regret my decision. Caring for the needs of a breastfeeding baby and for our family was in fact a fulltime job.

The first indication of my unrest surfaced when I became angry after someone referred to me as "not working." I retorted, "My job as a mother is seven days a week, twenty-four hours a day, with no weekends off!" Curiously, I felt compelled to defend my reasons for staying home.

Whenever Mark neglected to give me his full attention, I became dejected. I found it impossible to accept his suggestions concerning our home and child: I perceived constructive criticism as destructive. Our home was the only domain I could control, and I did not want anyone telling me what to do, even my husband.

I finally realized that I was reacting emotionally, defensively, and immaturely to Mark's genuine desire to be helpful. Since Mark was gone all day, his suggestions were a means of participating in nurturing Phillip. I decided that the immediate solution to this problem was to become involved in a community project, giving me an outlet for my creative needs as well as providing adult interaction.

I found my niche at the local public library where I began to volunteer for one and a half hours on a week night. This served a dual purpose, for it also gave Mark and Phillip time alone with each other.

Structure Through Goals

Stimulated by getting out of the house on a regular basis, I decided to take the initiative to direct my life's activities. Using two books, *How To Get Control Of Your Time And Your Life* by Alan Lakein and *Getting Things Done: The ABCs Of Time Management* by Edwin Bliss, I designed a career strategy. Step one was to list and define specific and professional goals, both short-term and long-term. (Seeing them in writing assured me that they were realistic and achievable.) Step two was to brainstorm and choose activities needed to attain each goal. Some goals would take years to attain, but dividing them into manageable tasks would keep me motivated:

1. To keep in good physical shape, I will take a two-mile walk, three times a week.

2. To remain intellectually stimulated, I will read at least one library book a month.

3. To develop a positive attitude, I will pay someone a compliment once a day.

4. To keep up to date in the field of dietetics, I will read at least one article from a professional journal a month.

My goals structure my life. Every day I prepare a to-do list which includes allotted time for a goal activity, in addition to the routine household chores. When overcoming a stumbling block, I reward myself with a nonfood item, perhaps a flower or a phone call to a favorite person. The ubiquitous stack of dirty dishes and dust get their share of my attention, but not all of it. As Alan Lakein suggests, I ask myself, "What is the best use of my time right now?" Answering this query helps me to disregard unimportant distractions and concentrate on dedicating my energy to meaningful goal activities.

New Direction

My career has not been halted; it has only changed direction. I now claim titles of mother, wife, homemaker, writer, community member, and volunteer. Already my list of advantages for being a fulltime mother is extensive. In addition to being my own boss, I have the time to enjoy the outdoors, and to pursue interests and hobbies, as well as to enjoy a less pressured lifestyle. Motherhood is not always glamorous. Sometimes its duties are a drudgery, but what job does not have undesirable parts?

My change in attitude has been a pleasant surprise. Now when I ask myself, "What do I want out of life?" the answer is no longer a puzzle.♥ © 1986

Susan M. Koshute, of Beaver, Pennsylvania, has three children, ages eight, six, and three. She enjoys growing flowers for potpourri and pressing them, walking, biking, listening to classical music, and shopping for bargains.

Multiple Me

*Are you kidding? I'm not
searching for identity.*

*Some plural definition maybe.
Why, there are pieces of me
emerging
all over the place,
talk about growth as a person –
I'd put a hydra to shame,
heads shooting from every fingertip.
Which person
do I grow as?*

Nedda Davis

Maternal Instinct
by Judy Lindquist

"Maternal instinct." The mere phrase conjures up images so universal that the words transcend country, religion, race, even species. It's a phrase that one never needs to explain: everyone knows what it means. Or do they? What does it really mean? How is maternal instinct different from, say, paternal instinct?

I recently pondered these questions when I realized I had developed very strong maternal instincts towards some eggs. Yes, eggs! Not your run-of-the-mill cooking eggs, but instead twelve fertilized eggs that had found their way into an incubator in my laundry room.

I teach morning nursery school classes in my home. For a science unit, we were hatching some eggs. This will be a good experience for the children, I thought, as we embarked on our month-long project. From the growth charts that we studied daily, we learned about the development going on inside the shells, development that we couldn't see but that we simply had to have faith was taking place. I began to feel toward these growth charts as I had toward the photos in the book *A Child Is Born* which I had studied while pregnant with my daughter. As the preschoolers and I made daily checks of the eggs' temperature (an exact 102 degrees was optimal), we made sure that the water tray was full to provide needed humidity and gently rotated the eggs. I was surprised by how strongly I began to feel towards the eggs. When the chicks finally hatched, I was as proud as any mother chicken would have been.

And it was with great sadness that I gathered up the unhatched eggs and put them in the trash. My husband smiled when I told him of these feelings. "But they weren't chicks," he said. Maybe not. But they had the potential to become chicks – and they had not done so. Maybe that is the essence of maternal instinct: the ability to see the potential of something, to see beyond the present.

As we hold our infants, we see beyond the tiny bundles that create mountains of laundry and that need to be bathed, fed, and clothed constantly. We realize the potential these babies have for growing, loving, and making a positive difference in the world. Perhaps that is what motherhood is all about: seeing the potential in our children and investing our time, energy, and selves in helping them to fulfill that potential, whatever it may be.♥ © 1988

Judy Lindquist of Orlando, Florida, a long-time contributor to **Welcome Home***, also writes for the* Family Journal *(a parenting magazine in Orlando). Currently the PTA president in her daughter's school and an active member of the Orange County Strategic Planning Committee, Judy knows mothers can make a difference in children's lives. A professional figure skater, she teaches several classes a week; her daughter Sarah, age ten, is one of her students.*

Being Parents

by Deborah Fallows

Editor's note: This is an excerpt from A Mother's Work, *by Deborah Fallows, published by Houghton Mifflin Company.*

The most important message I carry, after being a mother for almost eight years and after watching and listening especially closely to other parents and their children is simply this: parents are the most important factors in their children's lives. Whether they are with their children two hours a day or twelve, parents are special to children. They make the biggest difference during their childhoods. They make the most impact on the rest of their lives. I say this not with pride but with a humbling sense of the responsibility that being a parent brings.

Love Beyond All Bounds

The bond between parents and children is incredibly strong. The love between them is special: it grows for so many years without judgment, without limit. Parents simply love their children beyond all bounds, often as much for their weaknesses and their faults as for their strengths and gifts. I love that Tommy fights to control his temper as much as I love that he is brave and trusting. I love that Tad won't be dissuaded from his stubborn and unreasonable positions as much as I love that he is generous. Of course, I don't love the temper or the stubbornness, but I appreciate how these fit their personalities, and I appreciate how Tommy is fighting to prevail over his temper and how Tad will learn to give in one day.

Parents will do things for their children that no one else would dream of. You could ask a parent if he would cut off an arm for a child and without hesitation, even thinking, he would answer yes, and truly mean it. You could ask the parent about the rage she feels when someone does her child harm. It is not a normal rage that knows normal bounds. There is a depth of feeling, of commitment, of love, that lies beyond the rules of order of the rest of the universe.

Parents may carry these larger-than-life feelings about their children deep in their hearts, but most are never called upon to do extreme things for their children. Mostly we help them conduct their daily lives, help them with manners, with schoolwork, with habits, with their sense of right and wrong, of justice and morals. We help them in ways they can understand, through discipline, play, chores, explanations, and talking, and through example. Most of us, as parents, are forever interpreting our actions with our children in some larger scheme. "The kids set the table every evening; it helps them appreciate that someone has to make all these nice things in their lives happen." Or, "We can get a dog if the kids will feed him and walk him every day: they need to learn about the responsibilities that come with ownership." Or, "You can learn to shake hands and say, 'How do you do?' when you meet someone: there are certain signs of respect that all people show one another."

Most of the things we do with our children, like the things we say to them, can seem ordinary, small, mundane. But as I have lived with children and watched children in the company of both parents and caretakers, it has seemed to me that there remains a difference in the way that parents and caretakers approach even the small events of children's lives. At the playground, for instance, where I have spent countless hours in the last seven years, I have closely watched the dynamics of what goes on. I have watched mothers go up on a high and dangerous slide behind their toddlers and slide down with them, both getting grubby. I have watched nannies and sitters and their charges on the same playground. Their children will putter on the smaller slides and be pulled quickly away from the higher ones, for fear of danger if they venture near. I have yet to see a nanny or babysitter follow her charge up the slide and down.

At homes, I've seen and heard young children, maybe four or five years old, talking back to caretakers in ways I've never heard a child speak to his or her parents – at least not without provoking a reaction. The difference is not so much in the words as in the tone. "No, Maria! I don't mean those shoes. Bring me my pink ones!" And there is never a "We don't speak that way, young lady!" or "How do you ask for your pink shoes politely, dear?" or "Think again about how you should ask that question, Amanda," from the hired caretaker.

Staying Power

There's something else that's very special about families: their constancy and their staying power. Parents are the constant presence in a child's life. They are there well before and long after the usually frequent changes of the guard of caretakers. Housekeepers come and go, nannies put in twelve-month stints, day care center staffs will turn over regularly. But parents will always be there.

Being There

My observations bring me to a conclusion – perhaps not too radical and perhaps one that is quite obvious, but one I feel with strong conviction: parents, as the unique and special people in their children's lives, need to spend as much time as possible with their children. By this, I do not mean that parents should spend twenty-four hours a day with children. But I mean most of the time. It seems to me that a good babysitter for a few hours a day, a few days a week, is reasonable even for infants. I think that playgroups and nursery schools are wonderful for toddlers and preschoolers. I believe in kindergarten. I believe in school. But I also believe that children do best when they have parents available after school most days, if only to see for a few moments before they head out to play.

I think this message is different from the way we often tend to think about raising kids now. As adults, we are busy with our own lives, and we go to great lengths sometimes to "arrange" things for the children. We arrange babysitters, after-school activities, summer programs, Saturday sports, music lessons, special tutors,

amusements, and entertainments. Even parents of the youngest babies are picking up on the cues and signing infants up for tumbling lessons, hiring teachers to give them "lessons" with flash cards. There are classes, too, programs, projects for children of all ages.

Don't get me wrong. I do the same for my children, although perhaps a bit less of it than I used to. I think much of it is good – good for the children, who benefit from the exposure to a broad and expansive world, and good for their mothers and fathers, who through these activities meet other parents, gain some free time, or learn things themselves. But at some point, all these arrangements seem to take priority over what we should be doing: striving to give our children more of ourselves and more of our time. We're all busy; none of us ever has enough time to do all the things we need to do. We all need time for ourselves. But for this short period in our own and in our children's lives, we need those precious moments with our children, and they need them even more. I think perhaps we forget, in our rush and efforts to get more and better child care, that we should also aim for more and better time to be with our children.

Doing well by our kids doesn't mean buying them things, signing them up for camps, going on the greatest vacations, although all these things are nice. It means, most of all, giving them the sense that they are the most important thing we have, that we want to spend our time with them more than with anyone else in the world. Children, even young ones, are shrewd and perceptive; they can tell what we're doing. A baby will not know, if a parent is gone, what that parent is doing or why. She will simply know that the parent is gone. But a preschooler, even a toddler perhaps, will begin to pick up the clues.

We need to think hard about how our work as mothers and fathers fits into our own lives, as well. The feminists are wise to have taught us that all women need challenges, fulfillment, and satisfaction in life. All of us, men and women, have this deep inside us. But does this ambition have to be restricted to the world of paid work? At its best, work can offer a kind of spiritual satisfaction – a special feeling of achievement, a special wholeness, a sense that it is worthwhile, important, irresistible. This is a lesson about work from which women at home should draw. These are the elements of endeavor that women at home should look at – and they are the elements that, despite what the women's movement may choose not to say or explore, are indeed compatible with the major commitment of spending one's time at home raising children.

The boardroom or the corner office, where men have traditionally gone to search for challenge and reward and where many women are now following, are not the only places to find these rewards. There is at least as great a prospect of finding them at home.

There is an honor and legitimacy about being home raising children that parents – mostly mothers – KNOW exists. I am not talking about hollow words like "raising children is such a hard job" or polite comments about the "patience and stamina it takes to raise kids" that are spoken to fill space, without much understanding or concern. I'm talking about a sense that a parent has that for each child there is a life to help shape and that there is no one else who can do as good a job as she – or he – can. The honor and legitimacy of staying home to raise children will become clearer to everyone when more people show that they consider the responsibility too great to pass off to someone else. The moments of our lives are scarce and precious. When we show ourselves willing to invest them in our children's welfare, the effect can be immense.♥ © *1985*

Deborah Fallows lives in Washington, D.C., with her husband Jim and sons Tommy (fourteen) and Tad (eleven). In 1980, she left her job as assistant dean at the School of Languages and Linguistics at Georgetown University and has been a parttime freelance writer since then. She and her family lived in Asia from 1986-1990.

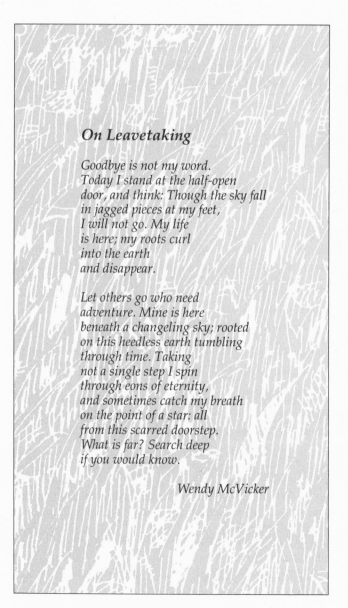

On Leavetaking

Goodbye is not my word.
Today I stand at the half-open
door, and think: Though the sky fall
in jagged pieces at my feet,
I will not go. My life
is here; my roots curl
into the earth
and disappear.

Let others go who need
adventure. Mine is here
beneath a changeling sky; rooted
on this heedless earth tumbling
through time. Taking
not a single step I spin
through eons of eternity,
and sometimes catch my breath
on the point of a star: all
from this scarred doorstep.
What is far? Search deep
if you would know.

Wendy McVicker

Unquality Time

by Linda Burton

When I was twenty-two and gorgeous, I saw this woman in the parking lot at the supermarket. She was driving a large station wagon, and she was yelling loudly at three disheveled children who had fudgesicle dripping all over their faces and onto their clothes. Groceries were spilling out of bags onto the back seat and floor. The woman's hair was uncombed and her clothes looked as if she had slept in them. With complete disgust, I pointed her out to a friend. "Ugh," I said. "I will never let *that* happen to me!" This unhappy-looking woman in the station wagon represented everything I never wanted to be.

At the time, I remember discussing with my friend how this obviously miserable woman would be a lot happier in an office. Her children drove her crazy, I suspected, and what she needed was a lot more mental stimulation. What her children needed, I thought, was a calm, loving mother. There was no question in my mind that she should "get a job and leave her kids with a sitter or something."

I forgot the incident until quite recently while in the car (a station wagon, as it happens) with my own children. I had had a sleepless night, dealing with the latest progression of flus and viruses which seem to adopt my children whenever the temperature dips below fifty-two degrees, and I was not in a good mood. In my rush to get out and pick up a new prescription at the drugstore, I had thrown on some soiled khakis and a T-shirt and had ignored my hair entirely, hoping I could just "shake" it into shape along the way. My thoughts were focused on the approaching evening.

Several months earlier, I had agreed to teach a few one-night classes for the county's Continuing Education Department. It seemed like a smart move. I thought teaching these classes would be a good way to keep up my professional resume – put on "hold" for the years I was raising my family – and get me into the world of adult stimulation. Best of all, the classes carried the extra bonus of requiring only a very small investment of my time. The day of the first class had arrived. Despite considerable advance notice, I still was not completely prepared. As I stuffed my overcoated children into their carseats, fussed with securing the various latches and locks, my mind was racing furiously ahead, trying to mentally tie up the loose ends of my class outline. Why did I ever agree to teach these classes?

Fear gripped me for a minute as I pictured myself standing dumbstruck in front of twenty-eight students, without an organized idea to call my own. These thoughts consumed all my attention as I wearily came to a stop at the traffic light signaling the edge of our community. Just at this moment, the eighteen-month-old decided to throw his bottle on the floor, jarring the top loose and allowing apple juice to flood the floor and creep under

the passenger seat. He screamed loudly for me to pick up the bottle. My three-year-old began to whine at a grating decibel level, and his brother screamed louder. The light turned green.

Angrily, I jerked the car over to the side of the road and lit into both children in a very unpleasant way. I had had it. My nerves were raw; my mind was flaccid from being pulled in spokelike directions; I looked terrible. I wasn't prepared for my class that evening. And at that moment, it felt like my predicament was all their fault. For what must have been a full minute, I screamed uncontrollable vituperation at my children. As I slumped against the car seat in exhaustion, I noticed that the traffic light had turned red again, and there was a girl – about twenty-two – in an MG directly opposite me. Beautifully dressed and looking terrific, she was staring at the picture I presented in horror and disgust. Our eyes met for only an instant before the light turned again and she went on her way, but it was a moment of complete insight.

I had become the woman I never wanted to be. I was the living caricature of everything that could go wrong with motherhood. I felt like there was only one place to turn. If being a mother was this exhausting, this draining – if it meant that my frustrations would make me turn on my children so cruelly – then I should go back to work. The mounting tensions in my life had caused me to be grossly unjust to my children, and nothing in the world

was worth that. Knowing that I had frightened them in the bargain made me feel even worse.

Maybe it would be better, I thought, if I were to go to work and hand the children over to someone kinder than I was, someone who was "better" with children than I was. Surely there were people who were "made" for the job of mothering; it's just that I wasn't one of them. Perhaps if I were away from my children for much of the day, I would appreciate them more at day's end. I wanted to feel good about myself as a mother, and it seemed at that moment as if the only way I was going to feel good was to turn over most of the job to somebody else.

But for the time being, the three of us were stuck together in a very small space, and we couldn't really walk away from the problem. Somehow, I had to disentangle us all from the frenzy of the last several minutes.

I apologized.

It was not easy, because I was feeling as victimized as they were.

"Look, guys," I said. "I'm really sorry I yelled at you. It wasn't right. I wasn't fair to you. I shouldn't have done it. Do you know why I was yelling?"

The three-year-old solemnly nodded his head. "You were mad," he said.

"Honey," I explained, "I wasn't mad at you."

"Then who were you mad at?"

"I don't think I was really mad at all; I was tired, and sometimes being tired makes you feel mad. Isn't that silly?" He didn't say anything. "But do you know what else, honey?" I added. "There's something I have to do that's kind of scaring me, and that made me act mad. Sometimes we act mad when what we really are is scared." He seemed to absorb the complex logic more easily than I would have thought. "Did I scare you, honey?" I asked. He nodded. "I'll bet I did," I said.

We discussed it a bit longer and we all seemed to feel much better as we continued our drive to the store.

At that unlikely moment, I made the firm decision to remain at home with my children. I knew no one could have taught them as much as I did in that car. I also knew that there was no job that could teach me as much as I had learned from them during that one incident.

What had they learned? First, they learned that it is OK to be mad. If my children saw me only during my "good" times and not my bad, how might they feel about themselves when *they* got mad? Second, they learned that when we don't do the right thing, there usually is something that can be done about it. We do not allow ourselves to continue repeating an unkind behavior. Finally, they learned that sometimes when we feel angry, something else really may be going on, such as fear or lack of sleep. I hope this episode taught my children to look occasionally beneath their own anger to see what else might really be bothering them.

From this very bad time – this supremely "unquality" time – I learned why it is crucial for me to be at home with my children. My purpose in being with them was to teach them how to live successfully, how to get through the vicissitudes of life as well and as happily as possible. I suddenly realized that I could not possibly teach them these important lessons if they did not see me go through some dismal times. I knew that my children would be examining carefully how I handled my own inadequacies to use as a model for overcoming their own.

So much of our success in life, after all, is measured by how well we are able to get through the times that aren't so good – the times when we are too tired, when we're frightened, when we fail. If we are not around to serve as examples for our children for how to get through those times and emerge victorious, then how will they learn the lesson?

Few of us, I learned, really are "born" for the job of mothering. Rather, being a good mother is a privilege earned through hard work and a continual daily recommitment to the importance of that work. It means being willing enough to confront the very worst in ourselves and brave enough not to run away from it when the going gets rough. In point of fact, mothering is rough and scary work. I understand fully how great the temptation is to hand the job over to somebody else – somebody "born" to do it.

Since that day at the stoplight, I have wanted to quit with great regularity. But then I never have begun a new job that I didn't want to quit periodically – especially when I was afraid that I was not going to do well. I would come home and say: "This job isn't for me; I'm no good at it. I'll never learn to do it." A real terror at the idea of failure always has made the idea of "giving up the ship" especially attractive to me. Unfortunately, however, whenever I have chosen to "give up the ship," I also have chosen never to experience the sea.

Sometimes I think that when we feel our most inadequate, we are presented with our greatest opportunity for self-revelation and growth. We are presented with an opportunity to take a chance on ourselves and come out on top – to build a confidence-reinforcing chain of success.

So I do not, at bottom, believe that mothers either are "born" for the job or not. We may be frightened of mothering. We may not feel up to it, we may run from its challenges, and we may call our fear a simple inborn ineptitude for the job. But then we never will experience the sea, and we never will see the view from the mountaintop.♥ © *1986*

Linda Burton is the mother of four children in Seymour, Illinois. She is a founder of **Mothers At Home.** *This is an excerpt from* What's A Smart Woman Like You Doing At Home? *by Linda Burton, Janet Dittmer, and Cheri Loveless, published by Acropolis Books, Washington, D.C. This book is available from* **Mothers At Home.**

Choosing Home

His Turn

by Robin Morris

It is three o'clock on a rainy Monday afternoon and I want my old job so bad I could scream. I want some place to go, some place out of this house. I want a reason to wear my nice clothes. I want to go out to lunch and not worry about the cost. I want to be respected for my abilities and paid for my accomplishments. I want the praise of other adults and a quarterly review to tell me how I'm doing.

"It's my turn," the song says, and today, in sweats and matted hair with a whining child, I'm ready to take it.

But this is just it, isn't it? It is not my turn. It must be the small child's turn. This is the time when they develop as persons; when the world becomes known as hostile or friendly, crazy or calm. It's the small child's turn, whether I've had enough of a turn or not.

Yes, today I want my old job so bad I could scream. But that's not bad enough to take Richard's turn (which is wholly in my power). My turn will come again, when Richard is older, and maybe then I will be able to appreciate my turn even more. Then again, maybe not. Maybe I will have missed out on my best working years after all. Either way, at this moment I have a more immediate, pressing engagement tugging at my pantleg, inviting me to a game of basketball rolling....♥

The Making Of A Mother

by Juanita Tamayo Lott

In Washington, D.C., the information capital of the nation and, perhaps, the world, there is one thing of vital importance nobody tells you – how to become a mother. At first, I thought it was a process of osmosis or immersion not unlike some crash seminars, workshops, or cassette courses many Washingtonians utilize to educate themselves on the latest policy issue or job vacancy.

My friends and I took what we considered prerequisite steps toward wanted and planned pregnancies:

- We married the egalitarian men of our dreams;
- We secured comfortable niches in the academic, private, or public bureaucracies; and
- We bought houses with backyards.

By the age of thirty, we were comparing lists of ob/gyns to avoid or interview. We knew of La Leche (of course, we would nurse our children!). We evaluated prenatal classes and reviewed the burgeoning literature on pregnancy and childbirth. We gave each other lovely baby showers and discussed how we would employ competent, reliable, and loving housekeepers for our four-month-old babies upon our return to the paid labor force.

What we didn't do was listen to our mothers; talk to seasoned and recent moms; take lingering walks in the local playgrounds; visit child care centers; or spend long hours with little children. In our ignorance, we eased through our first and second trimesters smugly.

Something, however, about the seventh month of pregnancy allows an inkling of doubt to surface. One begins to wonder how much she knows about the new life she will bring forth and to ponder her new role as mother. By the time she is wheeled into the delivery room, she realizes she knows about prepared childbirth but not prepared parenthood.

After the trauma of labor and the miracle of childbirth, I remember leaving the hospital with my firstborn. I was resigned to the fact that I would wear loose clothing home, but had not yet accepted the reality that the sleeping bundle in my arms was coming home to stay. The beauty of a newborn, fortunately, is that he doesn't give his mother much chance to dwell in abstractions or self-pity. I learned, or perhaps became programmed, to wake up half a dozen times in the middle of the night to pacify my baby's blood-curdling screams or catch his soft breathing.

Snuggling my child in my arms to feed him became second nature. And yet, at times, I caught myself wanting someone else to mother this tiny creature so I could go off to live my pre-mother life. I survived David's first three weeks with the thought that three months after his birth I was returning to the labor force and that my motherwork was coming to an end.

For a while, I was a blissful superwoman who had one child, worked fulltime, and had the services of a live-out housekeeper, doting grandparents, and a proud father. In my naive motherhood, I reached the incredulous conclusion that two children couldn't be any more work than one – just another diaper to change, another bundle to cuddle in the rocking chair.

Only with my second child did I come to realize how labor-intensive and time-consuming motherwork is. Two babies, fifteen months apart, turned out to be much, much more work than one. I took six rather than three months of maternity leave, minus a fulltime housekeeper.

In the winter of 1982, cooped indoors with my babies, I discovered I was very vital to two young lives, that I made a difference. This difference was as mundane as knowing exactly how long to warm David's bottle and as much of a nuance as holding him as long as it took to erase his insecurities of no longer being an only child.

I no longer worried about how my children were. I had no fears that they were being set in front of a television all day or that they were offered a drink only after hours of thirst. I was there when they woke, played, ate, cried, laughed, needed clean diapers, and went to sleep. I kissed them just for pure joy. Somehow, everything else at that point in my life was secondary to my children's wellbeing. I began to wonder: Did my children deserve any less than my full devotion? David and Joseph would be young only once. My being home with them during their formative years was a one-time opportunity of a lifetime.

Yet, it was not an opportunity I seized assertively. I was not ready to give up the rest of my life! I wanted the decision to stay home or return to work to be made for, rather than forced upon, me. All options – fulltime, parttime, or no employment – were open. My husband said he would support my decision fully, but that it was my decision and mine alone to make.

After what seemed an eternity (at least several sleepless nights during which I would tiptoe into my children's rooms and watch them sleep), I made the agonizing and somewhat surprising decision to remain home. The decision caught my friends and colleagues off guard. It relieved my mother, mother-in-law, and husband. It depressed and gladdened me alternately. There I was with two babies, eight bottle feedings and two loads of laundry every twenty-four hours. There were no more meetings or conferences to attend, no more projects to brainstorm or drafts to review. Gone were all moments of silence to myself to reflect, analyze, synthesize. It seemed that I had no identity but that of a fulltime momma.

It was a difficult first year on the job, but I learned many things–like being comfortable with my children and enjoying them for themselves. I learned to be kinder to at-home mothers and to listen to their words of wisdom admid constant interruptions from our children. (Actually, I discovered that the true interruptions were the things I did for myself, while my primary job was to lavish attention on my children.)

I came to a greater understanding of and respect for women who had made the conscientious decision not to bear children. I ached for the many, too many, women like my mother (not to mention fathers) who wanted to be home with their little ones but had to go out to work to ensure their family's livelihood. I empathized with women like my sister who needed their outside work to balance motherhood.

I wanted my husband home to be daddy, not so much to share equally the responsibilities of child care, but to enjoy our children as much as possible. I began to savor timeless moments to cuddle and kiss my sons, to talk with them and not have to run off and leave them. I began to think in terms of all children being my children, our children, whether they were in my neighborhood play group, at the local park, halfway across the nation, or in some Third World country growing up in poverty and civil war.

I marked my first anniversary of fulltime motherhood with more than a little help from family and friends who rejoiced in my motherhood but facilitated ways for me to keep up my involvement in other areas. I come into another year of at-home mothering realizing that motherhood has changed me permanently. Becoming a mother is such a humbling experience. More often than not, I wake in the middle of the night, if only to hear Joseph cough twice or David murmur a sentence and chuckle in his sleep. Physically, I am tired. I wonder what the record for postpartum depression is. I think my fatigue is due partly to reaching middle age, but I also can't help thinking that pregnancy, childbirth, and inadequate rest as well as lack of being able to take care of my needs first have taken their toll.

The word "mommy" continues to evoke a range of responses: ecstasy when my children enunciated it clearly for the first time; irritation when yelled at me in the middle of the night or during a tantrum; gradual ease when used as an introduction, as in "... and this is David's mommy."

In Washington, D.C., where people are made synonymous with their job titles and grade levels, I want everyone to know, especially my women friends, what my children taught me – that there's more to life than a career and that being a mother is an honorable achievement. I am learning to grow with my children and to face the ever-challenging stages of motherhood.♥ © 1984

Juanita Tamayo Lott, husband Rob, and sons David and Joseph, live in Silver Spring, Maryland. Using her expertise in demographic changes in American society, Juanita is sole proprietor of a home-based public policy consulting firm.

I'm Glad
I Can Be Home

by Jo Blasco

This February, it is nine years since I "retired" from my office job to stay home with my children. Actually, at the time I had only one – a son, nearly eight years old. His father died when he was under a year old, and he spent most of his early years in day care centers, while I struggled to make a living for us.

They were good day care centers – I wouldn't settle for anything less. They took a large portion of my very small salary. And when I got Danny home at night, I read to him and played with him. I gave him lots of undivided attention. But you know, it wasn't "quality time." I think it is a myth to say you can give quality time to a child after eight hours of work. I was tired and washed out. Many nights we ate TV dinners because I was too tired to cook. Although I read to Danny and played with him, I forced myself to do it. In spite of how dearly I loved my son, I really didn't enjoy him. I was too tired.

Those were the good days. The bad days were when Danny was sick. How sick does a child have to be before

you take off work to care for him? How many times can you call in sick and say, "I won't be in – my child is sick" before you don't have a job any more?

I was a secretary and a good one. I enjoyed my job. And I had to work to make a living. But it was not worth the price I paid. When my son was seven, I remarried. Three months later, I quit my job. I have never been sorry.

As I said, that was nine years ago. Now we have five sons and I enjoy them. I'm here when they need me, all day long. If they're sick, I can take care of them.

I've heard it said that at-home mothers don't spend quality time with their children. It's true I don't spend all my time doing things with the boys. Even if I could, I don't think it would be healthy. They need time to play with other children; time to ride their bikes, to build snow forts, to explore the woods behind our house. But I'm there to patch up skinned knees when someone falls off his bike, to admire the snow forts, to share the raspberries they find in the woods. And maybe that IS quality time, five or ten minutes at a stretch, all through the day.

There is another thing about being an at-home mother that means a lot to me. My children are not "latchkey kids" as I was. I remember vividly how scared I was, coming home to an empty house after school. Even the half-hour every morning between the time my mother left for work and I left for school seemed long. Although I was old enough (fourth grade) to spend a few hours alone in my own home, I was terrified, and my parents finally hired a housekeeper. Most families can't afford to do that. And it still wasn't the same as having my mother home. The two or three years that my mother was home were the happiest years of my childhood.

I'm building memories with my sons – things we wouldn't have time for if I were at work all day. I picked strawberries and wildflowers at a nearby farm last summer with my seven-year-old. We brought them home and pressed a sprig of the flowers in our nature book on the page that tells about them. We hulled berries all evening.

I grow a big garden every year, and every child old enough to squat next to a furrow helps me to plant peas, beans, and other seeds big enough for little fingers to grasp. Anyone old enough to tell the weeds from the vegetables helps me weed. When I can tomatoes, they fight over whose turn it is to crank the handle on the processor. The boys help me knead bread, fold laundry, make cookies. They teach the baby how to climb stairs. Sometimes they drive me crazy! But I have time to be with them, to enjoy them; time to store up happy memories for all of us.

I have time to be involved in my children's lives away from home, too. I've been a den mother for Cub Scouts, a room mother for kindergarten, a volunteer at the school carnival, the hot lunch program, and the Sunday school. I get a chance to see my children in a different environment from home, and so to understand them better.

I also have time to teach them the things I think are most important: the values that shape my life and will someday, I hope, shape theirs. There may be no guarantees to this business of passing on values, but even if children grow up to reject everything their parents stand for, I want equal time with the television, the newspaper, and the latest teen music idol. I have time to tell my sons what I stand for and what I believe. I have time to live out my values in front of them so they know that the things I tell them are not just ideals; they can be made to work in real life.

I've been talking about how great being at home is for me and for the children. But after all, it's my husband's paying job that makes this arrangement possible. So I asked my husband what he feels are the benefits to him of having me at home. He said, "Peace of mind." He knows our sons are well cared for. He knows if an emergency comes up, there is someone here competent to handle it. It allows him time to do his own thing: to play the guitar in a rock band, to work on our two cars. Sometimes we pile the boys in the car and go to a drive-in or go on a picnic and swim in a nearby lake. Or we get a babysitter while we take off for a few hours in our canoe. He doesn't have to come home and help me do the laundry or the cleaning; it's done already. We have time to enjoy being together.

So here I am, coming up on my ninth anniversary as a mother at home. Sometimes I feel like an endangered species! I read the magazine articles that say more than half the mothers in this country are off at work, and I feel out of step. I don't have any daughters, but I wonder if my future daughters-in-law will someday feel free to stay home with their children. I will feel sorry for them – and for their children – if they don't. There is great value for the whole family if Mom can stay home. And I wouldn't trade places with anyone else in the world.♥ © *1984*

*(Editor's Note: One of the biggest misconceptions perpetuated in countless media stories about mothers is that most of them are working. Please see "About **Mothers At Home**" for more information.)*

Jo Blasco writes from her home in South Haven, Michigan. She is the mother of Danny (twenty-four), Mike (fifteen), Scott (thirteen), Tommy (eleven), Patrick (eight), and Matthew (two). Jo is an active volunteer in several organizations, including a church support group for homeschoolers and a tutoring program.

Definitely Worth It!

by Mary Robin Craig

Just before their second birthdays, my twin sons spent the summer alternating between our backyard and the home of our day care provider. I was supposed to be practicing law part-time and spending two days a week with the children. One afternoon that typified this "perfect" arrangement stands out in my mind even four years later.

We all were out back when the telephone rang. I always encouraged both clients and colleagues to call me at home on my days off to discourage any notion that my availability might be less than generally is expected of attorneys. This time, the caller was a client, concerned about a deteriorating personal situation. I moved ten feet into the sunroom, from which I could simultaneously monitor the boys and converse on the portable phone. The warm and sunny afternoon slipped away as my client and I talked for forty-five minutes.

By the time I hung up, I was mentally exhausted. I sank down beside the boys, too worn out to play with them. Why, I wondered, was I investing so much time in other people and their problems? I felt a great deal of personal sympathy for this particular client – but there were dozens of attorneys in my city who could have assisted him. There was only one person who could mother my children.

A little more than a year later, I was waking up two or three times during the night to nurse my newborn daughter. As I held her while she drifted off to sleep, I found myself more and more frequently preoccupied with problems at work. I would look at my little girl's round face, trying to stamp upon my memory the tiny features that I knew would change so rapidly, and my thoughts would drift back to the office, to the brief that I was writing or to the phone calls that had to be made the next day. Again, I wondered, just what was I doing? There were thousands of attorneys in Cleveland. There was only one mother for this little girl and her brothers.

Yet the decision to retire from the paid work force was a wrenching one. I had spent three years in law school and eight in practice – a large investment of my family's money and my time. I was an associate in a firm that had hired me only three years earlier as a new mother of twins. A year later, the firm had agreed to try to work with me to assure that I could progress – albeit more slowly than a fulltimer – in my career and that I could remain on a partnership track; this was an unusual position for any firm to take, and would be so even today. Naturally, I felt that I had sizable obligations to the firm that had made a place for me. I also shared with other women who work in male-dominated professions a strong sense of obligation toward the other women in my field. If I were to retire, I would become one more statistic around which arguments are made in favor of limiting women's access to those areas of work.

However, it was becoming more apparent to me that I was unlikely ever to be able to forge that combination of career and family which I had anticipated. In my preparenting days, I had remarked in an offhand way to one of my superiors at work that I fully expected to be able to increase my work load gradually as my children grew. By the time they were in high school, I once again would be totally engrossed in my career. "Right," had been his sarcastic response. "They surely won't need you then."

At the time, I could not possibly imagine the commitment he and his wife had made to the thoughtful raising of their five children, and I blithely had attributed his remark to unrepentant male chauvinism. As my children get older, however, it becomes more and more clear that they do, in fact, need the constant involvement of their parents. When they are in high school – still twelve years away for my daughter – they will need to know that when they come home, chances are good that someone will be physically here and mentally ready to share their experiences, their concerns, their triumphs, and their defeats.

It was becoming obvious to me that I could not anticipate being both a sixty-hour-a-week trial attorney and the kind of mother I intended to be, not with small children and not ten years later. So why not continue to compromise? By bending a little here and giving a little there, as I already had done, I could avoid giving up all that I had worked for.

The truth? I missed my kids. I missed them terribly. And as they got older, I missed them more. I missed their imagination, their enthusiasm, and their yellow hair. Most of all, I missed the rhythm of their days.

Not the first steps or the first words (I never could determine which movements or sounds could properly be characterized as first steps or first words, anyway), but the pattern of it all, the pace – what I was missing out on was my children's own world. I got glimpses of it. On my days off, which often were broken up by errands (and telephone calls!), I could see that their lives had a flow that eluded me totally. From breakfast table to garbage pickup (large trucks) to sandbox to construction site visits (large trucks) to lunch to stories (about large trucks) to fire station visits (very large trucks), my boys plowed onward, chattering about everything, absorbing it all, and leaving me to wonder why I did not leave the court deadlines to others for the short time in which I could be surrounded by yellow hair and large trucks.

One December morning, my daughter four months old and my work load increasing, the seemingly endless internal debate finally concluded itself. I suddenly grasped that the partners in my firm and the legal profession as a whole had very little invested in me compared to what I had invested in my children. There really were a lot of people out there who could represent my clients. Only one person clearly would regret, twenty years later, having done that instead of having shared her days with three children who would be small for such a short time. As I began to say the words "I'm resigning" out loud – to my husband, to our nanny, to my supervisors and colleagues – I felt as if the whole world had been lifted from my shoulders.

Of course, it had not. Days with three preschoolers are not relaxing. In actuality, they tend to jolt along, not flow. They often are characterized more by frustration than by accomplishment. I sometimes think back to my office, where it was quiet and where even the angriest of individuals did not jump up and down screaming on a dirty diaper. But such an office (or an alternative) will be there later. This young family will not.♥ © 1991

Mary Robin Craig lives in Cleveland, Ohio, where she is an active volunteer at school, church, and with a hospice. Her twin boys are now seven years old and her daughter is four. She writes, "As a family, we enjoy traveling, camping, canoeing – and all kinds of other activities my husband and I would NEVER have thought of on our own!"

Time To Love

by Elizabeth Foss

It's late. I'm sitting in the rocker, my two-year-old son, Michael, tucked in bed next to Daddy. In the quiet of the night, I reflect upon the past year. A year ago, I discovered I had cancer. A year ago, my world was shaken to the core.

I had been a mother at home for a year after leaving a teaching career. "They" say a life-threatening illness makes one grateful for what she already has in life. And it does. But I was already grateful. I was so happy at home with a wonderful husband and dear baby. Now I am ever-aware of how precious life is and how important are the choices I make.

When I decided to stay home, our income was cut in half. I provided child care parttime to keep the budget balanced, and we thought we were struggling and sacrificing. When I began chemotherapy, we lost my income entirely and we added medical bills. We learned how little money we needed to survive, and we learned how generous our family and friends could be.

Before I became ill, I thought I spent a lot of time with my son. However, I also cooked, cleaned, did laundry, chatted with friends, and did all the countless things mothers do when they aren't exactly "mothering." During the course of my illness, I could do nothing but be still. I read countless stories, I played with blocks, I modeled playdough, and I watched "Sesame Street." I carefully observed my son being a child; I savored every delicious detail of his innocent play. While someone else did the cooking and cleaning, I was afforded the ironic luxury of doing nothing but spending time with my son. I learned how golden uncluttered time with Michael could be.

Other mothers at home always have been a great source of companionship. During a crisis, they are irreplaceable. Before beginning treatment, I had to wean a very dependent eighteen-month-old. Immediately. I couldn't do it "gradually with love." I had to do it all at once, with authority. Only another nursing mother (or Michael's dad) could understand the challenge. A good friend devoted days to helping me frantically distract a toddler who was begging to nurse. Only a mother at home could give of her time and energy the way that mom did.

Throughout my illness, other mothers contributed countless meals, many diversions, and babysitting services. It also was a mother at home who reminded me how essential I was and why I was fighting so hard. During a long hospital stay, my family and friends went to great lengths to assure me that my son was doing very well in my absence. Finally, a mom who had invited him to play with her children called me one morning at the hospital. "Oh, he is a good boy," she said, "too good. He's not his old mischievous self. He hasn't cried. There are no tantrums. But there is no spunk, either. He smiles, but he doesn't laugh." I searched for my doctor, asserted myself

as never before, and arranged to go home that afternoon. Someone needed me.

A life-threatening illness brings one a little closer to heaven. Before cancer, I always was mildly depressed upon reading the alumni magazine of the prestigious university from which I was graduated four years ago. What I was doing with my life never could be summarized into a neat paragraph among the business firms and law partnerships. Now I see with astonishing clarity that someone greater than the alumni officer someday will ask what I did with my life. I can think of nothing better to tell Him than "I nurtured my family with all my heart and soul. I devoted myself to their physical, emotional, and spiritual well-being." I think He will be pleased.

It seems my story has a happy ending. The disease is in remission, and my prognosis is for a long, healthy life. We hope to add to our family soon. My mother commented that I'll never be able to spend as much time with a second child as I did with the first. Perhaps not. But I don't know how much time I have. No one does. I do know that with each child I will give all the time that's mine to give. The only time I'm guaranteed is today. There is no place I'd rather spend that time than at home.♥ © 1991

Elizabeth Foss, twenty-five, is a mother at home in Springfield, Virginia, and a member of the **Welcome Home** *staff. She writes that her ever-optimistic husband encouraged her to write this article in order to see more clearly the silver linings around this cloud. They are thrilled to be expecting their second child soon.*

Perspective

*Lying on our backs
my baby and I
watch the fall leaves
fly through the air:
like golden finches,
they swoop and glide.
Trees meet above us
in turrets and towers;
a mobile of branches
catches the light;
a kaleidoscope of color
has fallen around us;
we are showered in gold,
coined and minted.*

*Look, through your eyes
I see
a carousel world
of magic and light.*

Barbara Crooker

Mouse Holes

by Penny Snyder

It was a stunning day, and I was sitting on a bench at the park watching my three-year-old son Jason. He was peeking behind tree stumps, looking for a mouse hole. I picked up the letter from a friend and read again the description of all her son was learning in preschool.

"And what is Jason doing these days?" The last sentence of her letter jumped out at me.

I picked up my pen and wrote, "Jason is looking for mouse holes," and then I giggled. It sounded so childish after reading about the little boy who was starting to write his name.

"Mouse holes" is a game, a silly one that Jason loves. One day I found a small hole in his pajamas, stuck my finger in and tickled him, saying "Mouse hole." This particular morning Jason wanted to find a real mouse hole.

I looked again at what I had written, and to me it looked just right for how a three-year-old should be spending his morning. I've felt the pressure for sending Jason to preschool. I've experienced the panic that my child will be behind somehow, unsociable, or too attached to me, but I'm happy to say the panic only lasted a minute. In resisting the urge to start Jason in school at three or four, he and I have gained a golden opportunity.

Jason is so different than he was at two: no longer a baby but a little companion. For the first time he has the chance to be an only child; his two sisters are both in school. Jason is discovering who he is as a person, separate and apart from me and the rest of the family.

Being home with Jason, I have at my fingertips all the time, creativity, and resources I wish to devote to him. The opportunity to teach is always present. If I do teach Jason, it is why the old maple in our yard deserves a respectful nod and why Bach is music for a joyous dance and Chopin for a more serious mood. There is plenty of time for learning matters of the world, but not nearly enough time to play.

What seems much more important than teaching is nurturing, which only I can do. If Jason hears a dinosaur, I can protect him from it. If we find a dead bird, I can comfort him. I am giving him a legacy he can carry with him forever – the gifts of the heart: my hopes, dreams, values, and love.

Jason and I have the greatest asset to any relationship: time. We have the opportunity for our friendship to blossom. I cherish the hours when we do nothing but cuddle, giggle, and tease – the childish hours. I can translate the million ways Jason says "I love you" because I know him so well.

For a small moment, Jason and I are creating our own world. We fill it with hugs, magic lions, sandbox creations, and right now, with a search for mouse holes. It is

a childish world and one that lasts for the blink of an eye. As I write my friend, "...our days are full and lovely, and together with Jason, the mice, and me, they are very happy indeed."♥ © 1988

Penny Snyder is the mother of Jenny (thirteen), Wendy, (nine), and Jason (seven). She is a freelance writer, the creator of the popular "From The Heart" department for **Welcome Home,** *and a columnist for her local paper in Salem, Oregon.*

Who's Going To Rock My Baby?

by Pauline Powell

Between my two-year-old's coughs and cries for a drink of water, my four-year-old's request for help to the bathroom, and the dog who couldn't wait until morning to be let out, I was up at least six times last night. And now the sun is up, much too early today.

I attempt a few precious moments of extra rest by having the boys crawl into bed with me. Jason, my two-year-old, likes to sleep, as he puts it, "top Mamma." That usually means across my chest or stomach, if I'm lucky. My luck runs out when he decides my face makes a more comfortable pillow. Chad, my four-year-old, is on the other side of me. He decides to have a kick boxing match with my rib cage. Fifteen minutes of this is enough! Let's just get up.

"Captain Kangaroo" is turned on in the hope that the kids will be preoccupied just long enough for me to shower and dress. Today I'm not successful. I do manage to shower, but not without Jason watching from the bathroom floor with a medley of "Done, Mamma?" and "Eat, Mamma?" Not yet, Jason.

Once dressed, we eat and I get everyone ready to face the day. I look around and see beds, laundry, dishes, floors, and two little boys, all needing my attention. It is only 9:00 a.m., and already I'm exhausted.

By 3:00 p.m., I'm feeling used and reused, unappreciated and maybe a little scatterbrained. I reflect back on my day and think, "I need to do something with my life. I have a college degree; I'm an educated woman. Why am I doing this to myself?" I pick up the paper in frustration, and I look at the want ads for the second time today.

As I read, I glance up to see Chad working intently on his newest puzzle. His shining eyes gleam with pride as he shows me his masterpiece. My praises are interrupted by Jason's whines. I scoop him up. I cuddle my cranky toddler and rock him with a soft hum.

I put aside the paper and ask myself, "If I get this job I'm looking for, who's going to rock my baby? Who's going to praise a job well done? Who's going to teach these children to live and love the way only I can?" I'm reminded that I **am** doing something with my life. I'm doing the most important job on earth. I'm creating and shaping the future. With renewed perspective, I stop and re-enjoy the simple and most beautiful gifts in my life. My sons!♥ ©1991

Pauline Powell, mother of Chad (five), Jason (three), and newborn Zachary, lives in Lewiston, Maine. She enjoys writing when she can and is an avid reader as well.

Jason's Trail

*Your one-year-old tracks are easier to follow
than footprints in the snow:
Instead of bread crumbs like Hansel or Gretel,
you drop Cheerios.
A trail of toilet paper here,
a shoe in the bathtub,
my cupcake pan on the bed – filled not
with yummy chocolate cupcakes,
but with the shredded leaves from one
of my favorite plants.*

*To anyone else, my house would seem
to be in a constant state of upheaval,
but to me it's only proof
of your busy life.*

*My paperback novel in the wastebasket,
discarded envelopes on the bookshelf;
your sister's jump rope in the closet,
the dust mop in her dresser;
Your stuffed clown gracing the diaper pail,
your rubber pants decorating the crib.*

*And at the very end of the trail –
if I follow carefully –
I find you, oh, what a treasure!
In your tiny hands are my address book
and the cheese grater, the very things
I've been searching all morning for.*

Penny Snyder

Mom, M.D.

by Kristi McClellan

At the age of ten, I set out to become a doctor. I prepared for and dreamed about a career in medicine. I also hoped and assumed I'd have a family some day. I firmly believed a woman could successfully combine a satisfying career with a rich and rewarding family life. The details of how this could be accomplished were rather vague, but that never troubled me. "It will all work out" and "I can do anything I want to do badly enough" were my mottoes.

My husband and I were seniors in medical school when our first child was born. We were thrilled with our little son, but I wished fervently that my vague notions about "things all working out" had contained more specific details. I took a six-month leave of absence and was very surprised how much I, a committed career woman, enjoyed being a mother and homemaker.

With four months of clinical rotations needed to complete my medical degree, however, I set out to locate that ideal child care setting. I started early with high hopes and higher expectations. The search was discouraging. I finally found a woman with whom I was satisfied (although her prominently placed wood stove bothered me), but she changed her mind about wanting to babysit. I realized at that point how unlikely it was that a paid sitter would have the devotion for my child and dedication to him that I had. As the date of my "return to the real world" drew closer, I was horrified to realize that my high standards for a caretaker were being reduced to "Will you take my son?"

In the end, my husband and I enrolled six-month-old Michael in a day care center, and life with "the best of both worlds" began. In some ways I enjoyed being back in the old familiar environment of the hospital. But so many things were different! The morning routine of nursing, feeding, and dressing Michael, then dressing myself, and finally packing a diaper bag left me exhausted before my workday started. I didn't have enough time to study because my evenings were needed for baby care. I didn't enjoy the baby care because I was tired, stressed, and preoccupied. Playtime with Michael was different because he was so drained after eight hours in a noisy day care setting. Michael was sick often, and I felt tremendously torn between my commitment to him and my commitment to my schooling. "What about my husband?" you ask. We smiled at each other in passing as we tried to keep up with laundry, shopping, and housework.

My husband and I soon decided that this two-career-and-a-family lifestyle was not for us. We were surprised to learn that the kind of home we wanted – a haven, a special place for us to be a family – didn't just happen.

That lesson has helped me understand how important my role as the homemaker is.

So it was that I received my M.D. degree, and embarked on my career as a fulltime mom. Do I ever have doubts? Sometimes. I have a good friend who is a mother of two and a practicing doctor; she's happy about her choice, and at times I envy her. But I have no regrets. I've seen how many little things each day influence my children. I'm so thankful that I can be with them to teach lessons through the everyday events, to comfort fears, and to model (on my better days) the qualities I hope they will develop.

The difficulties of motherhood certainly are obvious to me: keeping the clutter of two young children to a minimum is very discouraging. I clearly remember the tedium of endless hospital paperwork, though, and this reminds me that no career is without drawbacks. The remembered rewards of the world of medicine sometimes entice me: the intellectual challenge, the satisfaction of helping others, the recognition. Then my now three-year-old son tells his crying sister, "Don't be afraid; Michael's here," and I'm amazed at the magnitude of the reward I have in seeing loving, compassionate qualities emerge in this little person I am rearing. No regrets, indeed!

Just call me Mom, M.D.!♥ © *1987*

Kristi McClellan uses her degree from Baylor College of Medicine in caring for her husband Ross and her children Michael (seven), Karen (five), Jonathan (three), and Daniel (one). She enjoys homeschooling, swimming, reading, and of course, kids!

The Choice

by Veronica A. Joiner

It shouldn't have been such a hard decision, but it was. We had waited sixteen years for a child to come into our lives. After seemingly endless trips to doctors and hopeful visits to adoption agencies that ended only in more waiting and eventual disappointment, you would have thought the decision to stay home would have been easy once Mark was born. To this day, it remains the most difficult decision I have ever made.

Life was simpler in the old days when a woman was expected to stay home and rear her children. I don't say it was fair, but it was simpler. I fought for a woman's right to choose a lifelong career if she so desired. I still believe for some it is right, but just not for me.

I remember how guilty I felt when I finally announced that I would quit my career of seventeen years to remain at home with Mark. At one time a woman felt guilty if she chose to work outside the home. Now I feel that I am the rebel, the maverick, who chooses the very opposite.

The majority of my friends opposed the decision, as did my husband and his family. In all honesty, my husband was simply worried. We had been a two-income family throughout all of our marriage. The thought of being the sole supporter frightened him. Besides, we had begun breaking ground for a new house when we discovered I was pregnant. I knew my decision to be with Mark would shelve the house idea until I was able to work sometime in the future, or possibly cancel it altogether.

Added to the economic concern were fears over the loss of self-esteem and personal satisfaction. I loved my teaching career and after seventeen years finally had landed the grade I always had wanted to teach. Everyone told me I would regret leaving it. Teaching, they reminded me, was a perfect career to blend with childrearing. If I could suffer through the nine months while school was in session, we'd have the summer days to spend together; and, if I suffered through the first five or six years until Mark was in school, it would be worthwhile in the end.

I read every article, pursued every recent study proposed on the subject, and did a lot of praying and some crying, until finally I knew that the only way to be at peace with myself was to be a mother at home. I didn't want to suffer through those first five or six years of Mark's existence. I wanted to wallow in them.

Mark is two years old now and I have not regretted my decision for a second. While others rush off in the morning, Mark and I are cuddling together on the sofa, leisurely enjoying a glass of juice while we watch "Sesame Street." I look at the clock, recall my old schedule, and realize that instead of listening to and praising the learning efforts of another woman's child, I'm encouraging the newly acquired skills of my own little one. At the end of the day, when I used to be too tired to walk through the door of the house, Mark and I are making dinner and giggling at some shared joke.

My house is old and small, but it serves us well. I have learned that no house would be large enough to contain the love within our walls. My husband now enjoys the idea that I'm home and has come to realize that we can survive on his salary. Indeed, once the decision was made, he and his folks supported me totally.

I no longer feel guilty about my decision. All those years I spent arguing on the side of women's rights I was really arguing for a woman's right to choose. I chose: what I chose was the right to enjoy my son's childhood and the right to give him all the love and energy I once put into my classroom. One thing I know for certain is that I can always go back to teaching, but I can never go back to being with Mark.♥ © 1988

Veronica A. Joiner, a mother at home in Ridgway, Pennsylvania, taught in elementary schools for seventeen years, prior to the birth of her son, Mark. Her publications include a children's play, essays, and short stories.

Firstborn

You taste the warmth,
your cheek against my breast,
your tiny fingers
wound about my own.
And traffic in my mind
begins to slow;
your silent sleeping
chides my busy thoughts,
and all about us time
stands strangely still.

Where are the timely struggles
I should feel
in giving up my days
to watch you grow?
Perhaps they'll come,
but meanwhile, snuggled close...
this is the time
for whispered prayers
and dreams.

Valerie Bryant

Taking Care Of Ourselves

Songbird

by Robin Morris

It is 8:38 p.m., and Richard is singing in his crib. He has been there quite happily since about 8:10, and I have to wonder: what does he have to sing about? He is a mere sixteen months old, in the dark, and all alone.

On the other hand, why not sing? His belly is full, his bed is warm and dry, there are rumblings of Mommy and Daddy about the house, and he has the silky rim on "blanky" to play with.

I hear him sing from the next room and pause to listen. How delightful he sounds. And then I wonder: when do I sing? I too am alone, reading and writing and sipping hot tea in a comfy flannel gown. I too have my family about. Yet I do not sing. I work, I contemplate, I ponder, I suppose. Perhaps this is adult singing, but somehow it does not seem nearly so wonderful.

I consider how far gone I really am and realize that even making love I can occasionally drift to my list of things to do the next day. Pretty far gone.

It is not that I wanted to stop singing those lovely children's songs. It's just that life goes along, taking up my moments and my hours and my days.

When was it I was just reading..."What then shall I do this morning? How we spend our days is, of course, how we spend our lives" (Annie Dillard). I was feeling pretty good about that, now that I get up to spend my early mornings on productive things such as writing. But I am no longer so sure. I have to wonder, as Richard quiets into sleep, have I given something to my little boy that I somehow have failed to give to myself?♥

Lessons From The First Year

by Deana Mason

Today is my daughter's first birthday. It is a momentous day for both of us: for her, because it's a milestone of how much she's grown, learned, changed; for me, well, the reasons really are the same. This year has brought so much more than I ever dreamed: exhilarating joy, paralyzing fear, numbing fatigue, and infinite wonder. The year is crowded with memories too numerous to mention. I'd like to share three pieces of advice, however, with any new moms at home. They might be helpful to "veterans" as well.

1. Don't overclean. My mother-in-law, a wonderful, warm, lively woman, used to clean her baseboards daily when her children were small. She says now it was the dumbest thing she ever did. I've had to learn the same lesson. If I focus on the dusty furniture, chipped walls, cobwebbed ceilings, and smeared windows instead of on the delight of being with my daughter, I fret about the frivolous. Because I do have a tendency to be consumed by the quest for clean, I've had to train myself to ignore what everyone else already disregards. My daughter is not going to remember (nor care about) the state of the house, only the state of her mommy.

2. Don't overcommit. A legion of activities cry out for the mother at home's time and energy. Some may be necessary for a healthy sense of self-esteem. For me, this includes graduate school and church involvement. There are many days, though, when the best thing for my daughter and me is to stay at home alone and do nothing but be together. As a result, I've learned to say no even when it's extremely difficult, such as when a friend asks me to babysit for her children in a non-emergency situation or when my services as a volunteer are requested by a worthy organization (although I gladly say yes to either when it fits). After all, I quit my job so I could spend time with my daughter. Any outside activities can be life-giving; each mom has to decide for herself what's best for her and her family. Although I do have other commitments besides my daughter, by far the majority of my time and energy is devoted to her. That's my best fit.

3. Don't worry; be happy. Raising a child can be one "crisis" after another. Is she eating right? How should we discipline her? Are we spoiling him? Is she sicker than she looks? Should we call the doctor? Should we let him cry or should we always pick him up? Should we join a playgroup? Who's best: Benjamin Spock, Penelope Leach, or Burton White? I've found that most of my major concerns have turned out to be of minor consequence. This is not to downplay the vital need for responsible parenting, but there is no one way to raise a child, and no one is a perfect parent. I've decided to do my best, pray a lot, and leave the worrying alone. It's not easy, but it's a lot more fun!

With one year under my belt, all I can say is, "I can hardly wait for the next!" ♥ © 1989

Deana Mason is the mother of two children, Joy Marie (three) and Reid (one). She has just completed her Master of Liberal Arts degree. Deana enjoys music, writing, reading, cross-stitch, and sports of all kinds.

To Have And To Hold

by Diane McClain Bengson

In those first months, an infant seems to be always in arms. My arms. The months of constant holding seem to last forever. It was harder with my first baby. From the moment we came home from the hospital, THE BABY NEEDED TO BE HELD, and it was much more difficult than I expected.

I had read that babies needed to be held a lot and that it is important for their physical and emotional development. Intellectual knowing, however, did not help me with the day-to-day physical demands of having this baby in my arms from sunrise to sunset and beyond. (We had an infant seat, a borrowed baby swing, a bassinet, and a crib, but our baby didn't find these nearly as satisfying as Mom's arms.)

My baby wanted to be held almost constantly, and he let me know in no uncertain terms. I loved the feel of his skin and the wonderful smell of his neck just below his velvety soft earlobes. When he relaxed, his body seemed to fit mine like a puzzle piece. But I was quite unprepared to share my body so completely with another person and to rearrange the ways I did almost everything, from spreading jam on my toast (one-handed) to brushing my teeth.

Holding my baby slowed me down considerably. Simply moving from one place to another was slower: I just couldn't walk as briskly as I used to! Doing dishes, cooking, typing, and putting away laundry one-handed

took twice as long. And later, with two children, my greatest frustration became getting out the door. The baby often wanted to be held while we prepared to leave. I was always running late, and I needed to do lots of two-handed things quickly – tying big brother's shoes, carrying things to the car, and addressing an envelope that had to get in the mail.

But we learned to develop solutions. I adjusted to having so much physical contact with another human being, and I stopped getting that "touched out" feeling. I learned that I could do some things one-handed – like crack an egg, wash dishes, and write a check. But the greatest discovery I found was my baby carrier. "Holding time" became manageable with the baby strapped to my chest or my back. Though carriers have their inherent difficulties (such as finding one that's comfortable and right for you, getting a sleeping baby out of one or into one, and wearing the baby on a ninety-degree day), they saved my arms from aching and gave me two hands to use.

The slowness that evolved while holding my baby wasn't all that bad, either. I've been slowed down for a good reason: to focus on this brand-new life. But in twentieth century America, life is not slow! So I scramble to be both slow for my baby and quick to "keep up." The days I can accept the slowness are the good days – lots of holding, singing, and smiles all around. Surrendering to the slowness with a baby in your arms is one of the best places to find the enjoyment of a child's infancy.

Besides, holding is good for babies. The contentment they experience in arms, the better view they enjoy from up where the grownups are, and the gentle motion that promotes their inner ear balance and growth are all things I want for my babies. I also noticed that they were less fussy and slept better when they were held more.

The little-mentioned fact is that I know it's good and pleasant for mom as well. I've grown through holding time, and I have discovered energy, endurance, and love I didn't know I had. I love the feeling of having this small companion on my hip. Little compares with having a satiny head sleeping on my shoulder. These months are precious.

Then, suddenly, it seems to be over. Now, as baby number two is crawling and pulling up and nearing his first birthday, holding time has diminished greatly. I know there are still years of holding left – I'm still holding his five-year-old brother – but the constant holding is over. He'd rather be off investigating the stereo buttons and the crumbs dropped on the carpet. I'm left with sadness that he doesn't need to be in my arms so much. Looking back, holding time is so brief! In the end, the greatest thing is not the frustration, slowness, or awkwardness, but the tender moments that are far too short. ♥ © 1991

Diane McClain Bengson, homeschooling mother of Shaun (eight), and Joel (three), lives in Bellbrook, Ohio. An avid reader, she is also a cloth and basket weaver and enjoys gardening. Diane is a freelance writer and volunteers for La Leche League and other organizations.

Cries In The Night: Surviving Sleep Loss

by Laura Jones and Priscilla Walker

Strength doesn't lie in numbers
Strength doesn't lie in wealth
Strength lies in nights of peaceful slumber

Rogers and Hammerstein
The Sound of Music

A mother of eight recently wrote an article for our local paper about her youngest child's first day of kindergarten. How did she spend her first free morning? She went home and took a nap. She calculated she had been sleep-deprived for twenty years.

Sleep deprivation is one of the most common problems of parenthood. Even parents fortunate enough to have infants who sleep through the night from three weeks of age usually will go through some periods in which their children wake from ear infections, teething, croup, or nightmares. Some parents are faced with nights of trying to sleep in the hospital next to their asthmatic child or being awakened periodically every night by a child with a neurological handicap. Parents of teenagers may doze fitfully while they listen for a son or daughter to come in from a late date or the last shift at McDonald's. It is a rare parent who doesn't have some experience with sleep interruption or sleep deprivation some time in her parenthood.

In my own case, my wonderful nine-month-old daughter is a joy during the day, but wakes frequently at night, usually to nurse. The ultimate solution, of course, is to help her learn to sleep through the night (see box), but while we are working toward this goal, I am functioning every day on very little sleep. Though I manage to keep my family going, I know I have less patience with my three-year-old, less energy to accomplish my goals, and less resistance to cold germs that pass my way.

Everyone needs sleep to feel good and to stay healthy. But how much of our need is habit, and how much is truly essential? If we cannot get our standard eight solid hours, how much will keep us going? And how little will lead to physical and emotional problems? When we are sleep-deprived, how much rest does it take to recover? Sleep researchers still are working to understand sleep and the role it plays in our waking lives. To understand what happens to us when our sleep is interrupted, it is important to understand what happens during a normal uninterrupted night's sleep.

Normal Sleep

Through sleep studies conducted in laboratories since the 1950s, researchers have found that the average young adult goes through four to six cycles of sleep every night. Each cycle is composed of four different stages of sleep.

In the first three stages a person becomes drowsy, her perceptions shut down, and, over a fifteen-to-thirty-minute period, she gradually falls into a deep stage of sleep. The deep sleep stage is a critical stage of sleep, lasting about an hour in the first sleep cycle. The sleeper then climbs back into lighter stages of sleep until she reaches dream sleep, the other critical phase. The first dream cycle may only last ten to fifteen minutes. Dream sleep also is called REM sleep for the rapid eye movements that occur during this phase; all other sleep is referred to as NREM (non-rapid eye movement). Each REM/NREM cycle lasts about ninety minutes. As the night progresses, deep sleep periods become increasingly shorter and REM sleep periods increasingly longer. Toward the end of the night, REM sleep may last up to an hour, with almost all deep sleep occurring in the first half of the night.

What makes the deep sleep and dream sleep phases so critical? Deep sleep seems to be more physiologically important than any other phase of sleep. Researchers still are seeking to understand this phase, but it seems that the body revitalizes itself during this phase. A person who loses this phase of sleep will feel terrible physically. On subsequent nights she will compensate for the loss by spending more of her sleep time in the deep sleep phase. REM sleep or dream sleep appears to be more important psychologically. People deprived of REM sleep show changes in behavior and mental state, such as increased appetite, anxiety, irritability, and difficulty concentrating. Alcoholics and drug users do not have REM sleep at night. Severe cases of loss of REM sleep over several years may lead to hallucinations (waking dreams) during the day.

Circadian Rhythms And Sleep

In addition to these nightly sleep cycles, our bodies also follow a pattern of daily cycles called circadian rhythms (from the Latin "circa" meaning "around" and "dies" meaning "day"). Over one hundred biological factors, such as temperature, blood pressure, hormones, respiration, and energy levels fluctuate in a regular daily pattern. Most circadian rhythms fall into a twenty-five-hour cycle, which means that we must alter slightly our natural body rhythms to fit into a twenty-four-hour day. Most people can make a shift of about two hours plus or minus in their natural cycle without any sleep problems. Many people will stay up later than usual on Friday night and even later on Saturday night, while sleeping in on Saturday and Sunday mornings. (Parents seldom have this option!) By Monday morning, their sleep cycle has shifted several hours, making it difficult to get out of bed when the alarm goes off and contributing to the Monday morning blues.

Circadian rhythms normally are synchronized with sleep cycles. For example, body temperature is at its lowest point at night. When our temperature is high, we feel and function better. When it is low, we feel and perform worse. If awakened when our body temperature is low, we feel awful – not just from exhaustion, but

because our body temperature and other physical rhythms are at their low points, too. If we try to sleep later in the morning or to nap at an unusual time during the day, circadian rhythms geared toward activity and wakefulness may block us.

Quantity Of Sleep

How much sleep do we need? Seven to eight hours is the average for adults. The amount of sleep that is right for you, however, is part of your genetic makeup and your life circumstances. Your age, physical and emotional health, and lifestyle can affect the amount of sleep your body demands at different times. Though the total number of hours is important, how much sleep you can get at one uninterrupted stretch also is crucial. Dianne Hales, spokesperson for the Better Sleep Council in California, reports that people can function well for long periods of time on five uninterrupted hours of sleep every night, and that they do fairly well with at least three hours at a stretch. If you are awakened at more frequent intervals, your sleep cycles may be so disrupted that your sleep is not as beneficial to you as it should be. Having a night with sleep that is interrupted repeatedly has an impact similar to that of having no sleep. Although your body needs any sleep you can get, having interrupted sleep can lead to the same sort of fatigue and problems the next day as can having no sleep at all.

Interrupted Sleep

A typical night in a home with a child who wakes frequently may go as follows: around 8:00 p.m., you put your baby in the crib "for the night." You get your three-year-old settled in his bed and go to sleep yourself around 10:00 p.m. Just as you drift into your deepest stage of sleep, the baby cries, and you jump up to attend to her. When she is back asleep, you slip back into bed, only to be awakened by your three-year-old, who has a bad cough and needs some cough medicine. The baby wakes again at 3:00 a.m. and 6:00 a.m. At 6:30 a.m., your husband's alarm clock goes off, and soon everyone is up for the day. You woke easily some of these times, while at others you felt as if you were trying to surface from a very heavy blanket of fog. How quickly you became awake and how you felt depended on the stage of sleep you were jolted from, where your circadian rhythms were in their cycles, and how many nights of sleep loss you have suffered.

How much sleep loss is tolerable varies with the individual. Your life circumstances, your health, and the amount of physical and emotional support you receive from others all will influence how well you cope with long-term sleep interruption. It may not take much sleep loss for some of us to feel out of control, while others may manage for longer periods of time. For example, one mother of three in New Jersey was going through a very difficult time. Her friends and family began to worry that she was suffering a nervous breakdown, but her perceptive doctor suspected sleep deprivation. Once she started getting enough sleep, she recovered.

Another mother in Virginia lived with interrupted sleep for several years, claiming that she had learned to get by on less sleep. To some extent, her body adapted to the changes in her sleep patterns. Although you may adapt as she did to less sleep, it may be that you merely become accustomed to functioning with a little less energy and creativity. You may have less zip to your step and be a little less patient than you would be if you regularly got more sleep.

No matter how well you cope, however, losing sleep night after night will take a toll. According to Dianne Hales, the first casualty is your creativity. You will start to lose the ability to think flexibly. When making decisions, you will tend to go with the routine answers rather than try to think of new ways of doing things. You become more irritable, more moody, and less resilient. Motherhood is a profession that requires a great deal of creative thinking, whether you are coping with a colicky baby, an anxious child, or a teenager. Our children always are changing and growing; we need our flexibility and resilience if we are going to keep up.

Repeated nights of sleep loss or interrupted sleep also may lead to the loss of ability to perform certain tasks. Studies have shown that after more than one night of lost sleep, performance on tests and the ability to solve math problems or to push buttons in a specific order are impaired. Most mothers of newborns are not subjected to tasks that require such precision, but there can be dangers. You may turn on the gas on the stove and forget about it, or you may neglect to check the temperature of your baby's bottle or bath water, or you may not jump up to investigate the sudden silence when your two-year-old is on his own playing somewhere in the house. I once enjoyed a peaceful interlude of such silence blissfully. When I finally went to investigate, I found my two-year-old had gotten into the bathroom and put red lipstick all over the baby's face. I was lucky it was only lipstick.

Sleep loss can interfere with your driving. Driver fatigue is a major factor in a high percentage of traffic accidents. When you are sleep-deprived, the monotony and inactivity of driving long distances can make your body think it's a good time for a nap.

Even with decreased ability to perform routine tasks, it's important to know that a person functioning on little sleep almost always will rally in an emergency. If something does happen that requires quick thinking and fast action, a tired mother probably will cope just as well as she would with adequate sleep.

How To Cope With Your Own Sleep Loss

• Nap. Any amount of sleep is beneficial. Your body will strive to get what it needs, and even a fifteen-minute nap can help you get the basics.

• If you can't nap, rest. Find time to sit down, put your feet up, close your eyes for a few minutes, and visualize a calm, quiet scene.

• Make arrangements for your husband to take night duty occasionally.

• Try to plan to have a neighbor, friend, or other family member care for your other children so you can nap.

• Get exercise. It will help you relax and sleep better when you do sleep.

• Do something during the day to make yourself feel good.

• Talk to your spouse, family, friends, doctor, midwife. Communicating with other adults will give you a boost.

• Know that others have gone night after night without sleep, too. There is an end in sight. Eventually your child will sleep through the night.

• Work on your sleep environment by making your bedroom conducive to sleep. Use your bedroom only for sleeping and make it so quiet and restful that it becomes your sleep sanctuary.

• Remember that when you are sleep-deprived, your decision-making abilities may be impaired. You will tend to be less flexible, less spontaneous, and less original. You may want to delay making a major decision or defer to someone else until you get a good night's sleep.

• Don't take your fatigue lightly. Treat it as you would hunger or pain. It's a real biological signal. Make sleep a priority.

Helping Children Sleep Through The Night

How you deal with a healthy child's night waking will depend on what you see as best for you and best for your child. Some authors, notably Tine Thevenin, argue that we expect too much when we force young children to sleep alone. They recommend allowing children to join parents in a "family bed" so that children are secure and wakings less disruptive. (Tine Thevenin, *The Family Bed*. Garden City Park, New York: Avery Publishing Group, Inc., 1987)

Dr. Spock, on the other hand, follows a stricter policy. He states: "The baby has to learn that there is nothing to be gained by waking and crying. This can usually be accomplished in two or three nights by letting her cry and not going to her at all." (Benjamin Spock and Michael B. Rothenberg, *Baby And Child Care*. New York: Simon & Schuster, 1985)

Parents who don't want their children to feel abandoned at night but are unwilling to share their bed can find excellent guidance in *Solve Your Child's Sleep Problems* by Richard Ferber (New York: Simon & Schuster, 1985). His compassionate approach to helping children develop good sleep habits has helped many frantic parents and can be used with children of any age.

Spousal Impact

Every family has its own individual nightly routine with a newborn or for nighttime child care. For some, night duty falls solely on the nursing mother; for others, it is shared with the father. The decision as to who gets up in the middle of the night often is made on the basis of how much sleep loss the parent can suffer with minimal impairment to daytime performance. This may depend on a number of factors, including how easily a parent can fall back to sleep.

Even if a husband does not get up to tend to the baby, his sleep may be affected. He may get jarred into a lighter stage of sleep when the baby cries or when his wife gets out of bed. One husband may be able to fall back to sleep quickly, and another may be unable to go back to sleep as long as his wife is nursing or is out of the room. These men may lose sleep even though they don't get out of bed; of course, their sleep loss is not as great as it would be if they had risen themselves.

Children With Special Needs

It is comforting to know that a healthy newborn eventually will sleep through the night, but what if you have a child with a health problem that necessitates special care during the day as well as at night? Kathy, a mother of three in Ohio, shares her story of sleepless nights. Her eldest child has a severe heart defect and requires special care. Although Kathy has spent many nights "sleeping" by her daughter's hospital bed, she maintains that the hardest time of sleeplessness for her was not in the hospital. "There," she says, "you do what you need to do to pull your child through the crisis." The most difficult time for her was at home when her baby daughter refused to nurse and the doctors put her on a three-hour bottlefeeding schedule. Since the baby would not awaken herself, Kathy had to set an alarm clock to wake up and then struggle with feedings that her daughter, because of her heart condition, fought against.

Four-and-a-half years later, Kathy's daughter still requires nighttime feedings, though now through a tube in her stomach. Further nighttime care is required for Kathy's two healthy younger children. Kathy remembers that exhaustion coupled with stress was a devastating combination. She managed by relying on the help of family members – something that initially was difficult for her to accept. She strongly advises other mothers not to be afraid or hesitant to accept help from others.

Coping

Fortunately, your body is a wonderful machine that will strive automatically to compensate for the lack of sleep. You may become a more efficient sleeper, passing very quickly through the first stages of sleep in order to spend as much time as possible in the deep sleep phases and REM sleep phases. Dianne Hales highly recommends napping, as every minute of sleep you can get is valuable when you are sleep-deprived. "Sleep when the baby sleeps," is good, oft-told advice to new mothers. Unfortunately, this may be impossible when there are other children awake in the house or when your circadian rhythms are at their high point, dictating wakefulness.

Even when you do have a few minutes to sleep during the day, it may be difficult to decide to nap instead of grabbing that peaceful moment to clean the bathroom, make a phone call, or cook dinner. You should make a conscious effort to devote that time to resting. If you can't sleep, at least put up your feet and read for a few minutes. You will make it to bedtime in better spirits.

Recovery from sleep loss can be rapid. One good night can recharge your body and keep you going. Try to work out an arrangement with your spouse so that you can occasionally recover from your sleep loss. Some husbands may take over one of the night feedings, or others may tend to night wakings on weekend nights. An exclusively breastfed infant can be difficult to pass to even the most devoted father, but sometimes even such a child will settle back to sleep without his expected nursing, and you can catch up on some necessary sleep.

Remember that **your** needs are important, and that an occasional good night's sleep for you may give your child better days.♥ © *1990*

Laura Jones is deprived of her sleep in Falls Church, Virginia, with Nate (five) and Rachel (two). Priscilla Walker, who lives in North Potomac, Maryland, is the mother of Sarah (seven), Tommy (five), and David (one). The authors give special thanks to Dianne Hales of the Better Sleep Council; her insights contributed greatly to their understanding of the effects of sleep deprivation.

2 a.m. Feeding For Thea

Walking over the backs
of monumental insecurities
meeting you in the middle of the night

You become my little mother,
hand-signaling centuries
of accumulated family wisdom,
knowing what you need
and taking it (all from me).

There is a value in dreams,
in nights uninterrupted
by your open mouth, but

Once you were a seed
trusting me with
every cell division —
now I trust you
to wake me up
and tell me what I need to know.

Beth Joselow

Letting Dad Get Involved

by Karen Zwolenski

A friend who recently had a baby told me that even though she felt exhausted at the end of the day, she hovered over her husband whenever he changed a diaper or dressed the baby. She confided, "I found it difficult to let go those first few months. It wasn't that I didn't trust my husband or that my way was the right way; I just felt that our baby would be more comfortable if she were cared for by me."

It's not unusual for a mother to feel so protective. In order to get fathers more involved, mothers need to move aside and trust that fathers will do just fine.

How can a mother do this? And what can a mother do to encourage her husband's involvement? The following suggestions might help:

• Encourage your husband to feed and bathe the children, as well as change their diapers. This was, and is, a difficult suggestion for me to follow, but I'm working on it.

• Suggest ways that your husband can involve the children in household tasks. Children enjoy helping mom and dad wash the car, rake leaves, and prepare a meal. Everyone can benefit from a job well done.

• I've learned to refrain from giving my husband unsolicited advice. I can give him a chance to respond if I step aside. My husband has become more willing to "father" when I'm not hovering. He may not hold the baby the same way I do, but he does have a special touch, and our baby has come to welcome it. Also, I let my husband comfort our child's tears, and I allow him to do it in his own way.

• When I first became a mother, I looked forward to my husband's arrival home from work. Sometimes I didn't have to say a word. . . written all over my face was, "Please! Take her. I need a break!" But sometimes I noticed an irritated expression on his face. At first, we were too tired even to talk about it, but fortunately I picked up on his feelings and realized that he was tired too and in need of some alone time. Here we were, two tired adults, in need of respite from our baby. No matter what her mood was, pleasant or cranky, she had more energy than we seemed capable of handling. At first we quarreled about who was more tired! Finally we resolved to take turns for quiet time.

My husband and I each take a two-mile walk for our quiet time. It energizes us, calms us, makes us better partners for each other and better parents (less frazzled) for our daughter. Quiet time can be time at home or time away. Some suggestions: walking, swimming, reading, napping, letter-writing, participating in an exercise class.

But remember: our husbands are not babysitters! When I'm out without my children, if asked, I say that

SgSS ©

my husband is home with our children. I don't say, "He's babysitting!" When I hire a babysitter, she does not nurture my child as I would. Neither my husband nor I can be labeled "babysitters."

• Positive feedback works best when it is specific and timely. I encourage my husband when I tell him our daughter loved playing with him while I prepared dinner. By acknowledging his special ways with her, he's more likely to appreciate my efforts.

• A friend of mine is forever making lists, but that was something I had to learn to do. It's proven to be indispensable. (Sometimes I forget, but we all can't be organized all the time!) It helped both me and my husband to keep lists handy. For instance, in addition to emergency numbers, friends and family are listed near the phone; a list of the contents of the diaper bag is kept in a plastic bag inside the diaper bag, so either of us can replenish supplies; and a running grocery store list is put on the refrigerator so either one of us can make a quick run to the store.

It has taken a conscious effort on my part to involve my husband in the care of our children, and I'm glad I did; after all, we're a team.♥ *© 1988*

Karen Zwolenski, mother of Megan (five) and Lauren (three), is a fourth grade teacher. She and her husband Mark are able to share parenting responsibilities due to differing work shifts. They live in Northfield, Minnesota. Karen also wrote "Enterprising Woman" in this book.

Giving Our Daughter A Name

Stunned by the duties of love,
we thought how a name
makes a thing known,
lets us separate trees
from the tangle of forest
this is bay   this madrone
this black oak.
We thought how each word
is its own song
round   brittle   clear –
each its own call home
And we thought of the hoax
that words are, conjuring
objects out of air –
what makes it
water   paper   laughter?
How can a name
say all we mean?

Then, reckless as all
who love, we wrapped our hopes
in a few syllables,
gave to her a name,
a talisman, a single word
crammed with this blessing:

May you be fearless
and graceful,
bright as tears
and wise as wind.
May you delight
and understand, and
may you always be pleased
with your gifts

Hannah.

Jean Hegland

Breastfeeding: The Bountiful Benefits

by April Marie Heddleston

Seven a.m. Baby Joy is crying in her crib. I pick her up and bring her into my bed for her first nursing of the day. We both snuggle under the warm covers, enjoying the closeness and ease of this special time together.

Two p.m. Joy's big brothers wanted to go swimming today. After packing some food, cool drinks, towels, diapers, and sun screen, I am glad I didn't have to worry about bottles, too! We find a quiet place where she can nurse and then I take her to play in the pool. It is so simple and convenient, having the baby's food ready any time, any place.

Ten p.m. The baby and I sit down. While nursing, she reaches up to touch my face. I think she is memorizing every feature. She sweetly smiles up at me and then gets back to her meal. What tender moments these are. I treasure them. While nursing, she falls asleep, and I gently lay her in her crib.

Breastfeeding has bountiful benefits. But the special bonding between mother and baby has to be tops on my list. Convenience and ease are advantages that make it a combination that is hard to beat. Ruth Morgan of Warrenton, Virginia, who traveled to Germany with breastfed twins, feels traveling is much easier when the baby is nursed. She describes the benefits as less packing, no sterilizing, and no worries about cleaning and refrigeration.

Yet the health pluses for babies are what convince mothers like Sharyn Baer of Trumbull, Connecticut, to breastfeed. "I wanted to do everything right and give my kids all the benefits," said Sharyn. "What I read said breastfeeding was best." According to the joint statement of the American Academy of Pediatrics and the Canadian Paediatric Society issued in 1979, "the overall nutritional superiority of human milk remains unchallenged." Companies which produce infant formula are required by federal law to state on their product labels and literature that breastfeeding is best and is recommended for as long as possible during infancy.

Research has documented the many health advantages of breastfeeding. A nursing mother manufactures antibodies against the germs that threaten her baby and passes them on to the baby through her milk. Breast milk also contains living cells that act against bacteria in the infant's stomach. Breastfed babies have fewer allergies, fewer respiratory illnesses, and fewer skin disorders than do babies receiving formula. Breast milk protects against illness. Breastfed babies have less diarrhea, less vomiting, fewer ear infections, and fewer hospital admissions than bottle-fed infants. There also is less chance that a breastfed infant will suffer from constipation and dehydration. Breastfeeding also has been found to contribute to optimal brain growth.

Help When You Need It

New mothers getting started with breastfeeding for the first time are encouraged to get a book devoted to the topic of breastfeeding. Experienced mothers preparing to nurse again may find it helpful to have such a resource. I found that my favorite, *The Complete Book Of Breastfeeding* (by Eiger and Olds), came in handy many times. *The Womanly Art Of Breastfeeding* (by La Leche League International) is a favorite of many experienced nursing mothers. (See Books We Recommend, page 81.) Although your doctor, hospital, or other health care provider may provide you with breastfeeding information, support from mothers with successful breastfeeding experience along with thoroughly written materials can make a positive difference in your meeting the challenges of breastfeeding.

La Leche League International (LLLI), an organization established for the purpose of helping nursing mothers, has over three thousand support groups in fifty-six countries. Trained volunteer leaders can be contacted with specific questions. In addition, LLLI now offers a hotline: you can call to speak with one of their volunteers about any breastfeeding question or concern you may have. A good friend, relative, or neighbor who has breastfed successfully or who is breastfeeding also is very important as a source of support or information.

A new group of health professionals called lactation consultants is trained to instruct mothers with more complex problems. While they are of help in answering the routine questions about breastfeeding, these allied health care providers are able to help mothers and infants with special needs or problems such as breastfeeding a baby who is premature or born with a physical or neurological disability. They also can help when a baby becomes "nipple-confused." This confusion may arise when a bottle is introduced before a baby is nursing securely. (See below for information on lactation consultants.)

Meeting Early Challenges

New mothers often are unprepared for the realities of nursing. Early attempts to schedule feedings can interfere with the establishment of a mother's milk supply and undermine her confidence in her ability to nurse. This may cause her to quit breastfeeding before she and her baby have had a chance to establish their nursing relationship.

As one mother of four children recalls her first experience, "I was totally unprepared for how much a newborn would need to nurse and to be held. I tried keeping a time log to help me to determine a schedule. My experienced nursing friends helped me to understand that it was okay and in fact desirable to nurse frequently at the beginning. At three months of age, my son suddenly developed a regular spacing for most nursings. Now that I have four children, I have learned how different each child can be in style and need to nurse. However, the first three months is an intense and special time for a mother and child as they build a nursing relationship."

Jaundice is the most commonly treated problem in otherwise healthy babies, and it usually does not cause any longterm problems. Frequent nursing right from birth will help to control or prevent physiologic jaundice. In treating several of the less common types of jaundice, a doctor may suggest refraining from breastfeeding for a few days. However, it has not been shown that breastfeeding interferes with recovery from these jaundices, and interruption of breastfeeding can make it difficult for a mother to continue nursing her baby. In addition to consulting the doctor, do not hesitate to contact a LLLI leader if you have a question about nursing and jaundice.

Another problem that can be worked through successfully with the right information is mastitis, an inflammation of the breast. It frequently begins with a plugged milk duct which results in a tender spot or sore lump in the breast. While a plugged duct has a number of possible causes, fatigue, stress, or a change in routine often contribute to its cause. A low fever and flu-like symptoms also signal mastitis and its development into a breast infection. At the appearance of these latter symptoms, a woman should contact her doctor, who may want to prescribe an antibiotic and/or pain reliever. In both cases, treatment includes the application of heat to the sore area, rest, and frequent nursing to keep the breast comfortably empty. Since mastitis is not contagious, there is no harm to the baby to continue nursing, and the mother is more likely to recover quickly and without additional complications. Again, an experienced friend or La Leche League volunteer can help you through this experience.

I am glad I had the opportunity to breastfeed my children. It is one of the most loving, wonderful experiences that I can take part in as a mother and as a woman. As Sharyn Baer says, "You carry the baby for nine months. After he is born, it is hard to leave him. Breastfeeding is a special way to keep close."

Information: You can obtain the names of board-certified lactation consultants in your area by calling the International Board of Lactation Consultant Examiners, Inc., at (901) 755-6233.

You can receive additional information, support, and encouragement for breastfeeding from La Leche League International, 9616 Minneapolis Avenue, Franklin Park, Illinois 60131; 312-455-7730. The hotline is 1-800-La-Leche.♥ © 1990

April Marie Heddleston, mother of Jonathan (twelve), Chad (nine), and Joy (nineteen months), has taught elementary school. She now enjoys fulltime motherhood and volunteers as Early Years Editor for **Welcome Home.** *She is active in her church, where she is challenged by teaching Sunday school and leading a book discussion group.*

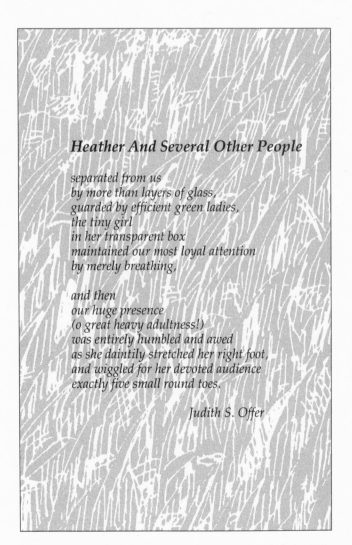

Heather And Several Other People

separated from us
by more than layers of glass,
guarded by efficient green ladies,
the tiny girl
in her transparent box
maintained our most loyal attention
by merely breathing,

and then
our huge presence
(o great heavy adultness!)
was entirely humbled and awed
as she daintily stretched her right foot,
and wiggled for her devoted audience
exactly five small round toes.

Judith S. Offer

Why So Blue?

by Dianne J. Moore

"In the hospital, everything was wonderful," my friend Judy told me after the birth of her son. "People visited me, bringing gifts and telling me how darling my son was. I was on a high. But five days later I sat at home, rocking my baby, tears streaming down my face, thinking 'I can't do this job. I absolutely can't handle all of this responsibility.'"

What my friend Judy was suffering from was the *baby blues* – an emotional letdown after delivery that results in tearfulness, irritability, mood swings, and fatigue. Between fifty and eighty percent of new mothers experience these blues shortly after birth.

According to psychologist Susan B. Campbell and colleagues at the University of Pittsburgh, up to twenty percent of all new mothers suffer a more debilitating condition called postpartum depression (PPD). The symptoms include anxiety, mercurial mood swings, loss of appetite, insomnia, and overconcern or lack of concern about the baby which, in turn, results in deep feelings of guilt. While the down-in-the-dumps baby blues typically last twenty-four to forty-eight hours, a PPD episode averages between six and eight weeks, but can continue for up to one year after delivery. Some women suffer *postpartum psychosis*, the most wretched torment of all. In a psychosis, an individual loses touch with reality. In some cases, women suffering from postpartum psychosis have harmed their babies, so the condition requires immediate hospitalization and psychiatric treatment. Fortunately, postpartum psychosis is rare. Only about one in one thousand new mothers experience it.

Physical Causes

"Everybody is different," explains Jane I. Honikman, cofounder of Postpartum Education For Parents (PEP) in Santa Barbara, California. "Some have the postpartum blues so mildly and handle it so well, they may have little or no symptoms except for some fatigue and low feelings. Others may experience tremendous upheaval and have to be institutionalized or put in a treatment situation because they simply can't cope."

The most common explanation for these postpartum disorders is dramatic hormonal changes in the body and brain before, during, and after childbirth. Says Leslie Feher, executive director of The Association For Birth Psychology in New York, "Pregnancy brings on increased levels of endorphins (the body's natural painkilling enzymes) in the placenta and in the bloodstream. It's possible that after birth, there is a withdrawal reaction to the reduction of endorphins similar to morphine withdrawal."

Other hormonal upheavals experienced by mothers include marked decreases in the female sex hormones, estrogen and progesterone, and changes in thyroid hormones and adrenal hormones which influence emotional states. Recently investigators discovered that some postpartum women have lower levels of the amino acid tryptophan, particularly at the end of pregnancy, and there seems to be a link between a lack of circulating tryptophan and the development of depression. In short, some women are physiologically incapable of adjusting to the vast hormonal changes following delivery.

Another physiological cause of the postpartum blues is drugs used during labor and after birth. "Oxytocin is a chemical administered to speed up labor and many women have a strong emotional reaction to this drug," says Leslie Feher. "Ask your doctor about this because there are other medications that don't have this side effect."

Other Influences

There's also a psychosocial aspect of the childbirth blues. For nine months, you've eagerly awaited the arrival of your new bundle of joy only to find that while caring for a newborn is exhilarating, it is also exhausting, hard work. You change wet clothes and dirty diapers, feed or nurse every three or four hours, talk, walk, soothe, and wonder if you will ever find the time to do laundry, vacuum, or catch an hour of much-needed sleep. If there are other children in your home, you also feel the need to give them extra attention and reassurance at a time when their security may be threatened. These demands produce pressures that can result in depression.

Jane Honikman says, "The whole focus of your life changes. You are totally responsible for a completely helpless human being. That change has a profound effect on your marriage and your sex life. You can't get enough sleep and you can't even have a conversation without being interrupted. Nothing is the same."

"This is why we see postpartum blues in adoptive parents, too," she continues. "A baby in the home is a change. Change doesn't mean something is bad; it just means something is different and requires adjustment."

Mothers who have had cesareans are not immune either, insists Leslie Feher. "For example, some women who have had cesareans tend to go through more depression after birth than women who have had vaginal births because they suffer a faulty sense of failure," she says. "The mother needs to understand that she has not failed by having a cesarean birth, or failed if the birth was not what she had fantasized it would be." Christine, thirty-two, who had an emergency cesarean, agrees. "I experienced a letdown because I didn't go through the whole birthing process. I still feel jealous and cheated when I hear my friends talk about their deliveries, but I know I didn't fail."

The Need For Support

Many parenting experts say that life stress and the absence of social support are the most significant factors in postpartum depression. When a mother has a good social network with friends and relatives, particularly an intimate and confiding relationship with a husband, she

fares better emotionally during the postpartum period.

"Unfortunately, many men have a bad reputation when it comes to helping with newborn infants," points out Leslie Feher. You might have a preconceived notion of the kind of support your partner will provide but find it doesn't materialize. He may decide to help by changing a diaper, find it's not so easy, get frustrated, and walk out on the whole scene. Or your own mother might try to take over caring for the baby, which could result in your feeling incompetent and resentful. "Recognize that your mate and family members might have their own needs and perceptions and try not to personalize that," she encourages. "Try to understand that, like you, they are also in the process of change. Then get all the help you can from those who can give it."

Your baby's behavior also can trigger the blues, says Susan Campbell. "Caring for a temperamentally difficult infant might increase stress in the postpartum period and influence depression." Says one New York mother, "Our baby started crying from 9:00 p.m. until 2:00 a.m. We tried everything – rocking, walking, swaddling, a pacifier – and nothing worked. I was extremely depressed until her crying tapered off." Again, a support network is vitally important at times like this.

Many people are astonished to learn that some men suffer postpartum symptoms, too. "Men who participate in the birth experience and who have a strong identifica-

tion with their partners tend also to experience endorphin highs immediately following birth," Leslie Feher explains. Furthermore, now the essential focus is on the baby. Different women have different ways of handling this. If you submerge yourself in the child's needs, which many new mothers do until they understand and are comfortable with the added responsibility of caring for a newborn, your partner may feel he needs to compete for your time and attention. The relationship then becomes one of jealousy and competition for affection. In other words, a new father may need mothering, too, and feel depressed until the roles in the family are balanced out.

But wait a minute. How much mothering can a mother do? Research shows that your capacity to nurture your infant requires that you also be mothered, coddled, and admired. Jane Honikman and four other women began Postpartum Education For Parents in 1977 because they realized they needed emotional support. Now there are postpartum support groups nationwide. "Everyone talks about birth and how to prepare for it," she explains. "Nobody talks about parenting. We as parents aren't being nurtured. We are told that we have to do the job and good luck. Prevention of the postpartum blues lies in letting people know they are not alone, and in helping them get some of their needs met, too."

Twenty-nine-year-old Karen agrees. "When I was pregnant, everyone took care of me. My husband was always telling me to 'take it easy' and the grocery baggers wouldn't let me pick up a bag. When the baby came, no one helped me clean up the messes or get up in the middle of the night. I went from being mothered to being a mother without help or instruction."

If there isn't a support group in your community, you can start one, urges Jane Honikman. For example, the support groups in California offer parent discussion groups, classes about the daily care of newborns, informal social gatherings, babysitting co-ops, and a twenty-four-hour, seven-days-per-week answering service. Those answering the calls are volunteers who can say "Yes, I understand you are having a terrible time. I remember. This is what I tried."

"One of our volunteers speaks to every childbirth preparation class," explains Jane Honikman, "and parents-to-be can sign up to receive a postpartum telephone call between five and ten days after they get home. At that time they are invited to join a discussion group in the community. We try to get the parents to feel good about themselves," continues Jane, "because then they can go on and handle the crisis."

Most new mothers experience some degree of the baby blues, from a few weepy days to a deeper depression; some even go on to postpartum psychosis. But help is available, so if you are going through the childbirth blues, be sure to reach out. It's especially important to seek help if postpartum depression lingers for more than two months, or if you notice signs of psychosis in a family member who recently gave birth. In these cases, don't hesitate to call your obstetrician or a mental health professional.

Resources

Postpartum Education For Parents (PEP)
P.O. Box 6154, Santa Barbara CA 93160-6154

Postpartum Support, International (PSI)
927 N. Kellogg Avenue, Santa Barbara CA 93111 (805-967-7636). PSI aims to increase the awareness of mental health related to childbearing, birth, adoption, and the implications for the family.

Depression After Delivery
P.O. Box 1282, Morrisville PA 19067 (215-295-3994). DAD's primary goal is "to support women who are suffering from postpartum depression and psychosis." It is also a national clearinghouse on postpartum depression and it distributes a quarterly newsletter. DAD is a nonprofit organization managed by volunteers and appreciates contributions to help defray expenses.

What Should Be Done?

The following suggestions may help you:

• Ask someone to stay with you the first week after you bring the baby home from the hospital.

• Take a catnap when the baby sleeps.

• Try to fit exercise into your day. Dr. Fred A. Stutman, author of *The Doctor's Walking Book*, says studies indicate that exercise may increase endorphins and norepinephrines. "These substances appear to have a mood-elevating effect and tend to give you a sense of well-being."

• Eat well-balanced meals. Mothers who breastfeed need two extra helpings of milk and five hundred more calories a day. If you're uncertain about your diet, consult a nutritionist.

• Try not to worry about housekeeping chores.

• Postpartum is a time when all mothers need extra help. Tell your husband and friends exactly what kind of help you need.

• Share your feelings of sadness with friends and loved ones who are able to be supportive at this time.

• Join a support group.

• Continue to visit with friends and family as much as possible.

• If you continue to feel depressed, get in touch with a mental health professional.♥

Dianne J. Moore is a fulltime freelance writer in Grand Rapids, Michigan, and a member of the American Society of Journalists and Authors. Her works have been published in over ninety national magazines and newspapers.

For My Toddler

Sometimes I feel soft and warm
like a pillow or a homemade quilt
I wrap my arms around you
and comfort you
You snuggle in
and get comfortable

Sometimes I feel hard and brittle
like an apple tree in the winter
you climb up on me
and I am afraid I will break
But I can hold you
and wonder of wonders
sometimes I even blossom

Cynthia Thomas

I'm *Not* A Housewife

by Renee Hawkley

I used to merely bristle at the title "housewife." Since our family bought a house with twenty rooms, however, I've crossed the threshold into militancy.

The trouble with being married to a house is the one-sided communication. A house won't listen to reason. It always has to have its own way. Do you think a house will listen to your side of the story when the bathtub doesn't get scrubbed? Not on your life. And it won't lift a finger to help out, either.

Talk about marital problems! There never has been a moment when all twenty rooms have been at peace with each other and me at the same time. While one room is whining, "Wash my walls and baseboards," another is wailing, "I'm lonely. I need the companionship of a $1,300 grandfather clock to complement my lack of personality."

Just when you get the walls to stop whining, the kitchen floor shrieks, "Get that soggy lettuce off me!" Besides being impossible to please, a house just won't let you off your hands and knees.

Have you ever tried to talk back to a house? The silent treatment can go on for years!

It's embarrasing being married to a house. People ask questions like, "Don't you work?"

I'm never prepared with an answer. Perhaps they think the kids and I go into hibernation from 8:00 a.m. to 5:00 p.m. and wake up to several stacks of clean laundry, a batch of oatmeal cookies, and a potty-trained two-year-old.

Of course I work! I simply make payments for the space I occupy on this planet by raising citizens instead of making money.

Then there's the problem of the forms....Whenever I fill out a form and write in "housewife" as my profession, I discover I have to leave the rest of the blanks empty. It's as if the term itself makes me as inanimate as the house is.

I'd just like to know where I was when the papers were drawn up and signed that wedded me to a house in the first place. One day I was a woman in love. The next day a house had staked its claim on me.

I've lived with lots of houses on a trial basis and seen thousands more. Maybe I'm just fickle, but I have yet to be introduced to one with which I would agree to share a marriage. The very idea of "tying the knot" with an address makes me feel like crawling under a lamp shade.

So I've talked it over with my real husband, a lawyer. Guess what? He doesn't like the idea of my being married to the house, either.

He suggested two solutions for a woman with my sensitivities. First, she could find a paid job. That might be interesting for a while, but frankly I can't take time off from work just now.

I like his other solution better, anyway. He assumed the role of judge, stood me in front of him, and said: "Repeat after me. I, Renee Hawkley...do solemnly divorce...the title of 'housewife'...and exchange it for...the title of 'mother.'"

Now that's a title I can do more than just live with. It's one I can love. ♥ *© 1987*

After twenty-three years as a mother at home, Renee Hawkley says it has been (and still is) "worth it [to be home] to have a good relationship with my children." She is the mother of six boys and two girls, ages twenty-three to six. With her three older children on their own, she now has more time for sewing, canning, and community service in Boise, Idaho. Renee, a longtime contributor to **Welcome Home,** *also writes for five Idaho newspapers.*

6-13-89

*All week I've wished you would
play more independently
so I could "get something done."*

now you are

and I can't

*I sit fascinated
intent on your every move
and expression.
enjoying*

My heart caught in your net.

Marcia Crosbie

Focusing In

by Laurel Cleary

The satisfaction we gain from being at home with our children is significant and very valuable to us as women and as mothers. However, that satisfaction often is tempered by irritations and frustrations inherent in the day-to-day realities.

So what does one do when getting out for dinner or a movie seems impossible? When even a walk in the park hand-in-hand with one's husband suffers a thousand push-me-pull-me-tie-my-shoes interruptions? When the view out of the kitchen window of scattered toys, toppled bikes, and that tall weed we've been meaning to pull out for the past three weeks is far more maddening than marvelous? How, in short, does one cope?

Lately I have found it useful to readjust my focus from the macro to the micro. I often am reminded, by family members and friends, that I ought to live one day at a time. That's good advice; the only problem with it is that sometimes one day can seem like an eternity to a mother such as I, at home with three active boys.

But why not further refine the concept? Why not practice living one moment at a time? Our days can be broken up into an almost infinite number of moments. No matter how active our children are, short periods of time are bound to be available to us, not for active pursuit of self-satisfying (and time-consuming) projects, but certainly for moments of reverie. I have found that such moments, especially when I am fortunate enough to be able to string several of them together at one time, go a long way toward restoring my peace of mind.

What exactly do I mean by this? What can one focus on in these precious seconds? The beauty of it is that possibilities abound, one or another of which is quite likely to be appropriate in almost any given situation. The ideas I mention are tailored to my particular interests; with a little thought, I know each reader will come up with ideas well-suited to herself.

I enjoy traveling, and I have been, in the years prior to becoming a mother, to a wide variety of places. Though I am unable, for both economic and logistical reasons, to go far at the present, I find that I am reminded constantly of places once visited and that I can, for that moment, revisit them in a very vivid way in my mind. Simply by focusing in on a particular subject – perhaps a tree or a flower I see while in the park, or a pattern of sunlight and shade I notice while out on a walk, or the roof-line of a building I pass while driving my son to school, or a cloud formation I spot while looking up (not down) out of that kitchen window – I suddenly might find myself taken back to another time and clime. Occasionally, a smell can be such a catalyst. I do not actively search out these associations, but I am open to their occurring. Often one will impress itself upon me when I most need it.

Then there is that impetus to reverie which does not trigger memories per se but rather acts as a springboard

for the imagination. Often I'll catch a glimpse of an interaction between two or more persons which will suggest to me an intriguing relationship. Some months ago, for instance, I saw an Indian woman, dressed in sari and sandals, and an Anglo woman, in wraparound denim skirt and white blouse, walking side by side, deep in conversation with each other. They have come to my mind many times since then, and I have spent some relaxing moments wondering about the circumstances which brought them together and what they might have been discussing. Of course, I'll never know, but the mental exercise of thinking about it for a minute or two takes me out of my situation for just long enough to give me a fresh perspective on it.

A favorite picture can have the same effect. I have a weakness for English country scenes. I have a couple of beautiful books, one with scenes from Yorkshire, the other of English cottages (both books were bought years ago, before financial constraints became part of everyday life), to which I go for moments of refreshment. If I haven't the time to search out a book, I might simply refer to a St. Patrick's Day card I picked up at the drugstore for a dollar that has a lovely photo of Kylemore Abbey in Ireland on the front. I keep it on a bookshelf in the family room for easy reference. It does amazing things for my spirit.

Music is another obvious tool to use in this way. Often around dinnertime, when the day is at its wrinkliest, I'll put on some music by Palestrina or Corelli, and I find even the most stubborn creases ironing themselves out. Just last night I tried an album called "Music of Shakespeare's Time." Suddenly I found myself sitting quietly in a walled garden, the shouts of my children becoming nothing more than the snorts of a noisy dragon under attack by a handsome (always handsome) knight in a neighboring dark forest.

One last suggestion I make is to take a few minutes to reread a favorite passage in a favorite book. I'm in the habit of copying down passages I particularly like into a notebook I keep for that purpose. Usually they are only a few lines long, easily reread in a brief moment, good for many minutes of reflection thereafter.

As you can see, the possibilities are endless, the relief to be had palpable. I highly recommend this moment-by-moment approach. I hope you will find the joy I have discovered, in the words of an obscure poet: "...peacefully grazing, our unicorn in the garden, waiting patiently, welcoming us to share." ♥ © 1990

Laurel Cleary, mother of Geoffrey (nine), Errol (six), and Peter (three), alternately mothers and daydreams, with a heavy emphasis on the former, at her home in Sutter, California.

Living With Changes

If You Can't Beat 'Em...

by Robin Morris

"It's just a stage," I told myself. "He will outgrow it."

But this particular stage seemed endless, and my rope was getting shorter and shorter. Finally, I broke down and called my sister-in-law, the one with four kids who knows everything about mothering. It was hard, admitting I needed help with only one child, but I was desperate.

"He's driving me nuts, Cathy," I moaned. "I can't even sit down in the same room or he'll crawl and poke and jab. It would be one thing if he sat still, but he cries and fusses and nothing makes it any better. I can't get anything done. I am going crazy! What should I do?"

"Embrace him," she advised.

"But you don't understand," I said, certain she didn't.

"Yes, I do," she said. "Embrace him. He is empty and unsure of your permanence, for whatever reason, and the more you resist, the more unsure he gets. The more unsure he gets, the more he will cling. Embrace him every time he wants you to, for as long as he wants to. Don't let go until he does. Eventually, he will."

It was the toughest advice I've ever had to follow, but it worked. And it made me wonder, was this also the secret to Cathy's happy and fulfilling motherhood? Might this same advice work one step further? I decided to try.

"Embrace motherhood," I told myself. "Yes, that very thing that is grabbing at you, extracting everything but the most minimal scraps of your former self. Embrace the craziness, the boredom, and the exhaustion. Embrace it, for as long as it takes."

This advice was not quite so tough to take, both because I was giving it to myself and because I really wanted to embrace motherhood. And miracle of miracles, it worked! The craziness is often an exciting pace, the boredom a chance to rest, and the exhaustion a symbol of work well done. As the saying goes, "If you can't beat 'em, join 'em." ♥

Mothertime

by *Diane McClain Bengson*

As I have grown into motherhood, much of what I have struggled with is time. Before babies and children, I had a neat, utilitarian view of life. I gauged time according to the tasks I needed to do, the leisure I desired, and the amount of time I required to care for myself. I often planned very active days, and by evening I usually accomplished all the tasks I had set out to do. Having a baby, I presumed, would add another element to my time and would fit neatly into either the "task" or "leisure" category.

But Baby did not. Baby had his own schedule and his own view of time. He did not sleep when I wanted to rest. He nursed when I wanted to sleep. He cried when I wanted to talk with a friend or get supper on the table. And he needed me all day long. Then Baby became a toddler and took an hour to walk a block while exploring sidewalk cracks, ants, and dirty candy wrappers. He wanted to eat at least ten times a day and "help" with the housework. He would bring me books to read when the spaghetti was boiling over and the phone was ringing. And then there was another baby!

My inner life was filled with constant conflict. Not until sometime during my second pregnancy did I realize that I had two choices. I could attempt to control my children and make them fit into my schedule; and on difficult days, I could have someone else care for them so I could do what I wanted to do when I wanted to do it. My other choice was to change my notions about time – to come to some understanding that would allow my children to have their needs and internal schedules met and also allow my own needs to be met to a sufficient degree, all the while *enjoying* the passage of time. This option led me to the idea of "mothertime" – a term I've coined from my own experience, but a concept that is useful for anyone who spends large amounts of time with children.

Learning To Deregulate

Learning mothertime was a slow process. My earliest lessons came during pregnancy, when I needed to find ways to rest more often and to slow down as my body became larger and more awkward. The waiting of pregnancy and the uncertainty about when this baby would arrive taught me the value of a new tempo – one that welcomed the unexpected surprises in life.

Soon after the birth of our second child, I began to learn that there was *enough* time. Maybe not always as much as I would have wanted, but certainly as much as we needed as a family. As soon as I stopped worrying about having time, I seemed to have plenty of it. This required lowering my expectations and reexamining my priorities. There was sufficient time if I didn't expect a perfectly clean house and gourmet meals. There was sufficient time if I took the children with me and avoided the places where we could not go as a family. There was sufficient time when my children and my husband were top priorities.

Being a mother around the clock was a lesson in itself. No longer could I see the distinction between being "on" and "off" work. Nor did I have a clear sense of what was work and what was play. Was doing the laundry "work" and caring for the baby "play"? If so, then was the laundry to be considered the "meaningful" part of my day? And if not, was taking care of my child my work? It seemed that caring for a sweet baby and a thought-provoking child was more pleasure than work, and even wiping dirty faces and picking up toys was not quite work. And what about my writing and reading that I squeezed in daily? Was that work or play? More and more, the neatly divided categories of work and leisure began to overlap. Even the clear distinction between "my time," "their time," and "his time" began to fade.

Life took on a rhythm instead of a schedule. In the mornings, after a quiet breakfast and journaling time, I usually moved quickly to do household chores, prepare the evening meal, shower, and dress the children. By mid- to late-morning, I was ready for a sit – which I usually spent reading to myself or my oldest child or else nursing the baby. After that, my day took on a slower pace, with an occasional midafternoon burst of house-work, followed by a restful period before dinner. The interval between dinner and bedtime was together time – for bathing, storytelling, crafts, or whatever we decided to do as a family. Then, if I didn't fall asleep, my husband and I would catch up with each other or I would read. The rhythm continued throughout the night, punctuated by dreaming and waking for night nursing.

In the midst of this greater daily rhythm, I began to notice many smaller rhythms. Breastfeeding, getting drinks, reading books, pulling apart Legos, going for walks, drawing pictures, checking on the children outside, and preparing them for sleep – each formed a little pattern within the larger one. This particular flow worked well for me. It felt good inwardly and shaped the day outwardly.

I also learned to use time in new, creative ways. Brief, concentrated periods of time became opportunities for accomplishing routine tasks. With the children happily occupied, I could rush through three rooms, pick up everything in sight, and then move the laundry from washer to dryer. The challenge was to learn to stop midrush when the children suddenly needed me. A variety of activities could be done in short chunks until they were completed: sewing, chopping vegetables, making bread, vacuuming, or adding thoughts to a letter that by evening would be ready to mail. The children's naptimes, on the other hand, became interludes for pursuing the things I most enjoyed: writing, one-on-one sharing with a child or my husband, resting with a child – anything but washing the kitchen floor.

A relaxed pulse is at the heart of mothertime. After all, being a parent means being leisurely enough to stop and look at the eighth daddy longlegs of the day, to nap in midafternoon when the baby does, to take a morning to explore the creek, and to wait while your child slowly and clumsily stirs the batter. Children feel that they have all the time in the world; to encourage their worldly explorations, we need to cultivate the same feeling in ourselves. Our culture does not encourage this perspective, but with a little planning – or better yet, unplanning – we can build a sense of timelessness into our day.

Timeless Tips

• Master the balancing act. Balancing planning and good time management with the spontaneity of living with children takes practice. You may find that being prepared to assemble supper in the morning eases the late afternoon grouchies. And yet, planning too rigidly or expecting to do an unrealistic number of tasks may increase frustration and cause you to respond less caringly to your children.

To balance the tendency to overorganize, consider the sage advice of professor, author, and former missionary Elisabeth Elliot: "Do the next thing." When faced with many tasks and responsibilities, choose the one that seems right for the moment. In times of clarity, "the next thing" may be making supper early in the day. In rare moments of more long-range vision, the next thing may be rearranging the living room. More often, however, the immediacy of the situation determines the best course of action. When the groceries need to be carried in from the hot car, the phone is ringing, and the baby needs to be fed, do the next thing!

• Give your children time, and trust that time is what they need. Children have their own timetables that cannot be advanced without serious compromise to their well-being. We need not worry about when our children will sit or walk because, given enough time, they will. Similarly, we need not worry about when to potty "train" or wean or teach our children to read. Children do these things when they are *ready* to. But if a particular developmental stage gets tiring or frustrating for you, rest in the comfort of the old saying, "This too shall pass." Our babies do not wake at night forever, and our two-year-olds usually lose their need to say no by the time they turn three.

• Develop a long-term sense of timelessness. It is essential to understand that the intense part of motherhood lasts for only a brief time. This segment of our lives may not provide many opportunities to see movies, to have romantic dinners with our husbands, read long books, do needlework, write plays, save the world, or work outside the home. However, early motherhood does not permanently banish these pursuits from our lives; it merely makes them unpredictable. Most of us will have thirty productive years left to devote to these activities once our children are older.

• Recognize that mothertime is incongruent with our society's sense of time – and honor the incongruities! When you are late for a dentist appointment because the baby needed yet another nursing, do not fret. Simply apologize. Time, in our society, is seen as linear – as moving straight ahead in a neat pattern. However, time with children is more zigzag: we do this, and before we finish we have done this and that, too. The interruptions are as significant as the goals.

I continue to grapple with time. It has a pervasive and insidious tick about it. But within the context of mothertime, I have found incredible freedom, new creativity, and a great way to enjoy my children and my life as it is now.♥ © 1990

Diane McClain Bengson, homeschooling mother of Shaun (age eight) and Joel (age three), lives in Bellbrook, Ohio. She has been published in a variety of magazines, and she volunteers for several organizations, including La Leche League. This article first appeared in Mothering *magazine, Winter 1990.*

The True "Expert"

by Martha J. Colaner

The first thing I did after finding out I was pregnant with our first child was go to the library. Then to the bookstore.

Throughout the pregnancy, I tracked the baby's development, the physical and emotional changes I was going through, and the feelings my husband might be having. I pored over first-hand accounts of labor and delivery (even though the accompanying photographs terrified me). I studied list after list of helpful hints for the layette, for breastfeeding – anything that had to do with the magical world of newborns.

After Katie finally made her squalling entrance in the delivery room, my appetite for knowledge increased yet again. I read Dr. Spock's *Baby And Child Care* practically cover to cover! I really became obsessed with the experts' analyses of the various "stages of infancy." Like all first-time parents, my husband and I were endlessly fascinated with the popular milestones: turning over, smiling, sitting up, and crawling. The books and articles I read told me what to expect, how to respond correctly, what not to do, and how to cope with typical problems.

In short, Katie never went through a phase, stage, or period unanalyzed.

For all this intense observation, the most amazing thing of all happened without our even noticing it: my baby turned into a person. While my husband and I were busy commenting on our child's current stage of development and anticipating what was to come, there evolved a bright, precious little personality. She developed a marvelous sense of humor and a troublesome stubborn streak, among other traits. Most importantly, without my witnessing it, she developed the purest sort of love for her parents – a love based on absolute trust and unconditional adoration.

I still read up on stages and phases, but less often, and with a more critical eye. Experts' advice reassures and genuinely helps first-time parents, but I've learned that I am the foremost expert when it comes to my child. Further, I've realized that the thrilling part of raising children is rarely even tangible, much less capable of being measured and compared. Right now, the most thrilling part is the emergence of a person. Since I'm the prime expert in the field, my instincts will be best able to deal with the stubbornness, to encourage the sense of humor, and to guide the person my daughter is becoming.♥ © 1988

Martha J. Colaner is a freelance writer and editor who is at home with her daughters Katie (five) and Erin (three) in Cincinnati, Ohio. Active in a babysitting co-op, Martha is a classical pianist, and she enjoys reading and walking. She is the author of a children's book, Julia and Grandma Peaches.

Switching To Fulltime Motherhood

by Elizabeth M. Ours

*Editor's note: Among the **MAH** staff members, we have women with widely different needs and tolerances for structure. It's another reminder that there is no one "right" way to be – we enjoy our differences. Most of us still are fine-tuning our approach to planning and structuring our days – after all, our families change each year as the children grow. We think Elizabeth's article will give you some ideas you can experiment with. Just remember that as soon as you think you've figured out when to fit in your morning shower, the baby will change his sleeping patterns (if he has any in the first place). Don't give up! Flexibility is a well-earned mothering skill, respected and understood by mothers everywhere.*

As with any major change in your life, the switch from being in the paid workforce to being home with your baby can require a significant period of adjustment.

These tips are intended primarily for the time following the first six weeks to three months after your baby's birth. During those first crucial weeks, your main priority should be to get to know and adore your baby and to recover from childbirth. When you begin to feel settled and start longing for some order in your life, it's time to implement some of the following strategies.

Dressing For Success

Just as your previous career required a certain style of clothing, so does your new endeavor. Purchase some inexpensive, comfortable, easy-to-care-for clothes that suit your new activities.

You're probably accustomed to getting up early each morning, taking your shower, and getting ready for the day. This simple routine suddenly is disturbed when a baby enters the picture. You now may find yourself waking up and feeding, burping, bathing, dressing, and playing with the baby. Suddenly you discover it is 10:00 a.m. (or later!) and you're still in your nightgown. Don't despair. There's still hope!

It may help to have a flexible plan for getting back in a routine of showering and dressing as early in the day as possible. You may want to find some shortcuts since your free time will be fragmented. For example, I've opted for a hairstyle that can be left to dry by itself because I often don't have the privilege of showering and styling my hair in the same time slot. But if I can get my shower out of the way, my new, easier to manage hairstyle can be "fixing" itself while I attend to my children's needs. I find that getting up ahead of the rest of my household to attend to my own needs pays off in providing me with a much better attitude towards myself and my family members and their demands.

Managing Your Time

A baby can be so demanding that you may find an entire day goes by and you feel you've accomplished nothing. Remind yourself that nurturing your baby is the most important item on your agenda.

On days when you seem to do nothing else but care for your baby, at least write down what you did do, such as "rock baby," "walk with baby," "change baby," "feed baby," "play with baby," and "bathe baby." It may make you feel better just to see something concrete on paper.

You may find that a significant block of time is now hard to come by. You might not be able to relegate housecleaning to one weekly three-hour time slot, for instance. Instead, you might try dividing up the tasks or rooms involved and plan to accomplish a couple of items each day. Your house will never be totally clean on any one day this way, but neither will it be a total disaster.

Make a list of the things you need to do and assign each item an estimated completion time. Then when you suddenly find yourself with fifteen minutes while your baby is catnapping or sitting quietly in the infant swing, you can accomplish something and check off one of the items on your list. The action of checking off item after item is great for your sense of accomplishment, so write down everything!

Decide which items on your list are most important to you and then do them first. Also, don't waste time doing something while your baby is napping that could be done with the baby awake. Ask yourself, "What's the best use of my time right now?"

Scheduling Your Days

Because life with a new baby can be so hectic, I often found myself floundering even when I had some general goals in mind. So I developed a system for scheduling my days. I bought a small spiral-bound notebook and turned it into an appointment calendar by writing each date and day of the week on a separate page. Now I spend a few minutes each evening before going to bed planning the next day. I write everything in my little book: household chores I plan to accomplish, appointments I need to keep, the names and phone numbers of friends I want to contact, milestones reached by my children, menu plans and items needed at the grocery store, upcoming events, special projects I would like to accomplish, personal and professional goals, just about anything I need to know or do. This one idea has greatly helped me to organize my life, plan my days, and use my time more efficiently.

Setting Goals

In your previous job you may have structured your days by setting short- and long-term goals, establishing priorities, and devising a plan to accomplish them. This method also is great for the new mother at home. Identify what is important to you now and what you want to accomplish in the long run, then bring these long-term goals down to monthly, weekly, and daily goals.

Goals can be anything, from attempting to have the house in order by noon each day, to finishing a home improvement project you started last fall, to starting a new home-based business. After setting your goals, develop a step-by-step plan for meeting them. In addition to the things you'll accomplish, this is great for your mental health. When you're endlessly rocking a colicky baby, your mind can be a whirlwind: planning things you want to accomplish, thinking of home-based business ideas, "writing" articles to be later put down on paper, and more.

A word of caution: don't get so carried away with your plans that you forget why you're home in the first place. Remember that your priority is always that new life who is so dependent on you. Some days you just won't be able to accomplish a single thing other than caring for your new baby. But there will also be days when things go smoothly and the baby takes an unusually long nap. On those days, dust off your action plan and get going.

Evaluating Performance

A frequently missed aspect of new motherhood is the positive feedback and encouragement that are part of a paying job. You must learn how to be your own best boss now.

Take your list of objectives and goals, make sure each one is as concrete and measurable as possible, then schedule regular performance evaluations. Weekly, monthly, quarterly, however often you decide, sit down with yourself and honestly look at how you met your objectives. Don't be too rough on yourself and remember to reward yourself with a suitable substitute for a raise or promotion.

Developing Your Skills

In your previous work you probably spent a certain amount of time reading trade journals, learning new skills, and participating in training classes or furthering your education. Putting the same kind of energy into developing your skills for your new line of work may help you get started. For example, you could subscribe to parenting magazines, read books, and attend seminars.

Networking

You need to develop a new network. To find it, go where the mothers are – parks, malls, libraries, mothers' support groups, and more. Develop a network of mothers with whom you can discuss concerns you may have about your baby and about being a mother; or whom you can ask for advice about colicky babies, sleeping through the night, the latest techniques, baby equipment, and more. Since new mothers often feel isolated without the adult contact they had in their former jobs, this network of friends is even more crucial now that you're staying at home. In fact, the support of friends going through the same things often will seem to be your only link to sanity.

Scheduling Time Off

Most jobs provide a couple of days off each week and a couple of weeks off each year. Motherhood does not. You're at work twenty-four hours a day, seven days a week! This can be overwhelming! You're only human – you do need a break from time to time. Perhaps your husband will care for the baby a certain amount of time each week while you pursue activities that rejuvenate you; perhaps you can find a babysitter or mother's morning out program. Many mothers take turns watching each other's children. Search until you find the outlet that is right for you, but don't neglect this vital break. You'll run out of gas if you never refill your tank.

The Bottom Line

Don't ever underestimate the skills that a successful mother/homemaker perfects: self-discipline, creativity, flexibility, time management, organization skills, the ability to communicate and motivate and train others – the list goes on and on. All of these are skills that are highly valued in the business world. Never sell yourself short; being a successful mother is no easy job, and in the end it reaps rewards far more valuable than any paycheck!♥ © 1990

Elizabeth M. Ours is the mother of three children: Tiffany (six), Ashlyn (four) and Taylor (one), in Spartanburg, South Carolina. She homeschools Tiffany and is the founder of a local support group for mothers who choose to stay at home. A former technical writer, Elizabeth puts her skills to work now as a freelance writer.

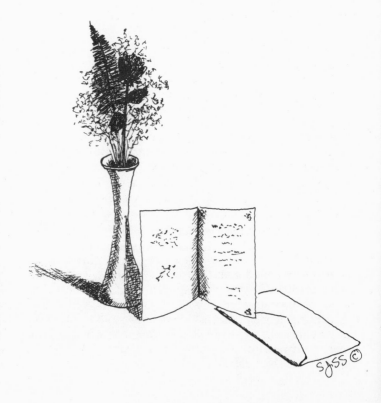

Chronicles Of Love

by Mary Fisk Docksai

One of the most rewarding aspects of being a mother at home is being there to share the moments, events, milestones, and humor that life with our children brings. In the process, we find that we are in the business of making memories, for our children and ourselves. We have no trouble preserving the major moments, in writing and on film, but often it is the day-to-day growth and experiences that are even more special. Recording those memories is a wonderful way of saving them. Our children benefit as much as we do: when reviewing these chronicles of love, they realize anew how special they are to us. Here are some ideas for capturing family memories.

Moments To Cherish

Making permanent records of her children's charming moments came naturally to Deanne Dixon of Potomac, Maryland. She describes herself as "a record keeper" who enjoys keeping journals.

Deanne bought an inexpensive binder-type notebook with a plastic cover, intended to catalog the family's special moments. "We started out with one for everybody, but it soon got out of hand and we now have one for each child."

She recommends recording the events and sayings in chronological order. She also suggests having one book for the family as a unit in addition to individual books for each child. "It is important to each of my children to have his own book, and each one likes to get his out and go through it. The children go through one another's as well."

How does Deanne find the time to make the entries, with five children of her own and a day care business in her home? "I have the books handy in the kitchen 'where the action is.' I know if I don't make myself write things down right away, I won't get back to it. I do it immediately." She cautions, though, that "it is important that the child does not know that you are writing down the event and his comments. He will become self-conscious and you will lose the spontaneity of what is going on."

Deanne started each child's book when he was very young. The first months are filled with notes about what that child did or what developmental progress he made. In addition, Deanne records typical moments from each child's life. The following are examples:

Daniel. _When he was five, Daniel cautioned a visitor about keeping a respectful distance from his sister, then age one._ "If you don't leave Debbie alone, she will beat you up because she knows baby karate."

Eric. _At age four, Eric and Deanne were going over a list of prospective party guests. Eric said,_ "I don't want to invite him." _Deanne asked,_ "Why not?" _Eric explained,_ "Because he always cries when I hit him."

Debbie. _Debbie, then age five, was watching a Cinderella tape with a neighbor, Mark. She admired Cinderella's ball gown, and she asked Mark,_ "Don't you wish I had a dress like that?" _Mark grinned, hesitated, and then said with all the tact at his command,_ "I like what you have on now better 'cause you can climb trees in it."

Deanne adds, "The best times have been when we are all together at the dinner table when Dad reads the stories aloud and we feel very close. Once the children get past the shy stage, they love to hear the stories about themselves. It helps them to realize that they truly are precious."

Long-lasting Journals

Mother of six, Cynthia Lynch of Hingham, Massachusetts, keeps one book for the family with the official title, _Out Of The Mouths Of Babes_, but she refers to it most often as _The Joke Book_.

Cynthia approaches the technical aspects of the book as enthusiastically and diligently as she does its contents. She offers the following practical suggestions designed to produce as permanent a record as possible:

Paper: "A blank book with sturdy, sewn-in binding and good quality paper, preferably in white and unlined, is best," she says. A ring binder can be used, but a small size is preferable. "Do not use regular notebook paper; acid-free paper, the weight of cover stock, with 100 percent or very high rag content, is best. Xerographic paper in bright white holds up well, also." She suggests that prospective journal keepers can purchase good paper and have it bound by a bookbinding service.

Writing and drawing instruments: "It is nice to be creative and decorate your pages with color or original designs," Cynthia points out, "but be wary of washable ink, which can be ruined easily by small spills, wet hands, or drools. It is best to use a ballpoint or cartridge pen with permanent ink. Washable ink from felt-tipped pens is easily smudged or damaged by water; felt pens with permanent ink bleed." She feels that color is acceptable for decoration, but finds black ink is best for writing because colored ink is more difficult to read and may fade. In addition, colored ink does not photocopy well.

Cynthia recommends using permanent color markers, crayons, colored pencils, and decorative ink stamps to draw. She stresses the tendency of permanent markers to bleed through the paper, and she suggests that if you want to use them, you write on one side only. She points out that using stickers or pasting things to the page is unwise unless you use permanent archival paste, since most glues dry and crack with age.

What and when to write: Cynthia urges, "Write things down immediately if possible." If she cannot write down the incident in the book itself, she will jot down notes and the punch line on a scrap of paper and stash it in the book to be transcribed later.

"Always be on the lookout for possible entries," Cynthia advises. "And I don't forget Dad's words of wisdom or funny situations that might come up."

Many Ways To Capture Memories

Julie Huettner of Rochester, Minnesota, began keeping a journal the day she discovered she was pregnant.

For this permanent record, she chose a hardcover, bound, blank book. She did not establish any set routine for writing in it, other than adding entries after visits to her obstetrician. She simply wrote "whenever I felt the urge to record thoughts and feelings." In addition, she noted Bible verses which were especially meaningful to her at the time, entries about childbirth classes, and a list of layette and nursery items. Julie ended her pregnancy journal with a final entry about labor and delivery.

For her son's first year, she kept a monthly log of eating, sleeping, and playing habits in his baby book. On a calendar she recorded daily happenings, such as when he smiled at Grandma. She also has a hard cover blank book for recording thoughts and interesting facts about him. In addition, she placed birthday and holiday cards in a box, "waiting to be pasted into a large scrapbook."

Julie finds that collecting photos is another method of capturing memories. She used both studio portraits and snapshots, dating each photo, with a separate album for each.

"I've found that it's nice to have a separate snapshot album for my son, so that when he is older I won't need to rob the family photo albums or search through old negatives to make an album for him," she says. She labels all negatives and stores them in the safe deposit box.

Julie began *My Book Of Birthday Letters* on her child's first birthday. Using a blank paper book with approximately twenty-two pages, she writes to him "each year on his birthday, describing my son's personality, likes and dislikes, and facts about our family. Someday I will present this book to him."

Julie already has encouraged her son to enjoy his early memories. When he was about three months old, she made a book for him called *My Book*. She cut tagboard to approximately 7" x 10" and put a special snapshot on each page: his first photo, Mommy, Daddy, grandparents, the cat, his house, his cousin. She wrote a sentence on each page and covered the entire page with clear plastic contact paper and tied the book together on one end with cord yarn. She says, "My son would smile and laugh as I read to him. Now he can name everyone on each page."

Family Journals

In Melcher, Iowa, Teresa Blasi's entire family participates in journal keeping, each member recording thoughts, feelings, and attitudes.

Teresa suggests you can start the journal at any point in your family's development, whether the children are babies, toddlers, teens, or college students. The kids can design the cover.

She believes the journal should be kept in an accessible place, such as the kitchen, the family room, or the car. She recommends that plenty of pens, pencils, crayons, and markers be stored near the journal. Some families prefer to tie a pen to a piece of string and attach it to the journal, while others prefer to have all the items in a small box.

Teresa urges family members to feel free to write anything and everything in the journal. If children are too young to write, they can draw pictures or dictate stories. Teens can write about sporting events or music concerts. Other entries can include important events, favorite jokes, and funny statements.

Time Well Spent

The possibilities, styles, and techniques for preserving memories are as unlimited as they are fun. The time you invest in designing, implementing, and maintaining a system that is right for you will bring a rewarding return of memories and moments in the years to come.♥ © 1986

Mary Fisk Docksai, Herndon, Virginia, the managing editor of **Welcome Home***, is the mother of two children, ages nine and four. She enjoys reading, writing, and volunteer activities.*

Tips For Journals

• Include snippets of local, city, national, and international news.

• Encourage your child to write his name or draw a picture every few months.

• Add stories or poems written by your child.

• Record notes or quotes from teachers, family members, and friends.

• Encourage your husband to make entries.

• Tuck in tales from your own youth, employment experiences, and special interests.

• Feature the thoughts of grandparents.

• Consider a looseleaf binder with plastic pockets to save birthday cards and mementoes.

• Once in a while, keep a log describing ordinary activities for a few days – it provides a "snapshot" of everyone's interests.

Name Calling

by M. Regina Cram

When I promised to love, honor, and cherish for better or for worse, no one told me about naming the baby. My husband and I suffer from a common marital ailment: incompatibility. A look inside our closets best reveals our personalities. Peter's closet is lined with "semi-dirty" socks (What, may I ask, is semi-dirty?), clothes worn twenty years ago, and items which somehow lost their way enroute to the hamper. His gravestone surely will read, "You never know when it might come in handy." In contrast, my motto is, "If it does not move within twenty minutes, throw it out." We once had a neighbor who arranged his shirts in alphabetical order by color. While I am not quite that compulsive, I do thrive on law and order. It is a wonder that our marriage survives.

Given our basic incompatibility, I should have anticipated that naming our children would be impossible. His family relies heavily upon lineage; my family has so many fruitcakes that we try to avoid most family names. Peter likes traditional names (read "dull"); I prefer unusual ones. At this writing, we have only days remaining to agree upon a name for our third child, and unfortunately the task does not get any easier.

For a boy, we began with the traditional look at fathers' and grandfathers' names. That yielded Wilbert, Harkness, and Sidney, among others. So much for that idea. Ancestors offer us totally unwieldy names like Jehosophat and Ebeneezer, or ones that are disastrous with Cram, such as Samuel. Would you send a child into a schoolyard with the name Sam Cram?

We have pored through books of names, genealogy charts, war memorials, and Bible stories. One day I scoured the credits at the end of a cartoon to get ideas. But the conversation is always the same. My husband doesn't want "Colin." I don't want "Jon." He doesn't like "Caleb." I know too many "Michaels." He knew an obnoxious kid named "Owen" but had a terrific friend named "Buttons." The only "Buttons" I ever knew was a neighborhood dog who chewed my favorite stuffed lamb when I was six years old. And so it goes....

Of course, other factors beyond personal preference come into play. The relatives become increasingly vocal with each pregnancy, realizing that this may be the last chance to name a child after Uncle Melville or Great Aunt Bertha. Our four-year-old has suggested the name "Poochie"; the two-year-old prefers to name the child "Meredith," in honor of herself. Only our dearest friends offer us the consolation that no one ever registered for junior high with the name "Baby Cram."

So, night after night, the negotiations continue. Always the planner, I grow increasingly anxious as the days pass. On the very day that I made a packing list for my hospital stay, Peter said that he has little motivation to settle the issue because the discussion was too theoretical. I suggested that perhaps if my contractions were two minutes apart, he might feel more of an incentive. It is apparent that even our four-year-old is aware of our growing desperation, because yesterday he offered to let us use the name of his bear, Big Teddy. When Peter asked how we could distinguish between the two, Skip was appalled at his ignorance. "Daddy," he sighed, "The one with the fur will be the teddy. The one without the fur will be the baby!"

All the while, it grows increasingly likely that soon we will announce to the world a Pam or Sam Cram.♥

© 1990

We are relieved to announce that negotiations were successfully concluded and the Cram family members welcomed Elizabeth Tierney (now two) into their Glastonbury, Connecticut, home. Since then, Louise Victoria (two months) has joined Skip (seven) and Meredith (five). Regina enjoys bicycling and letterwriting. Her "dream" is to continue developing her freelance writing skills while being a mother at home.

Family Arithmetic

When we two
added one
and became three,
the time sufficed.
I had enough
for spouse
and son
and even self.

But when we three
added one
and became four,
the time divided.
I had to balance
demands
and dreams
and duties.

But, oh, the love —
the love multiplied.

Alecia S. Lyons

Dollars, Sense, And Motherhood

by Arlene Rossen Cardozo

Kay Arnold left her $25,000 retail sales position last fall to stay at home fulltime with her new baby. Ruth Willmar took a longterm leave without pay from her suburban Los Angeles nursing post for a similar reason. Joan Bomberg, once on a partnership track with a prestigious Boston law firm, is now at home mothering, as is Andrea Lewis, a former Minneapolis receptionist. These women and thousands like them from coast to coast have temporarily traded office and paycheck for home and playground, a trend for which I have coined the term *sequencing*.

Sequencing runs counter to the recent practice of a mother's working outside the home throughout her adult life to contribute to the family's support and/or to realize personal goals. Viewing one's life as a sequence of phases, a married woman's decision to leave her career for a period of years to raise a young family can make sense – both emotionally and financially. And with this option has come a widening of part-time work opportunities for sequencing women who want to resume career activity as their children grow but who wish to postpone fulltime work until later.

To couples contemplating sequencing, the foremost question is: How can we afford it? When I began research for my book *Sequencing*, I assumed that the higher the husband's salary, the easier it would be for the wife to leave her work for a period of time if she so desired. I couldn't have been more wrong! Instead, I found some families where the husband earned over six figures who said they could not afford the loss of the wife's salary. At the opposite pole, some wives had left their jobs to be at home with their children despite the very low level of the husbands' earnings.

In almost every case, sequencing is a values decision. If the couple really wants the mother to be at home with the children for a period of years, they find a way. The allocation of their financial resources becomes the implementation of their underlying values decision.

Decisions on sequencing occur at one of two main junctures: 1) months or years before the first child is born, in which case the sequencing is planned long in advance; or 2) after the first or second child's birth, in which case the sequencing is unplanned. Clearly, planning ahead makes the financial aspects of sequencing much easier to handle than waiting until a child arrives and a standard of living mandating two incomes has been established.

Planned Sequencing

Brian and Kay Arnold of Chicago knew from the time they were married – four years before their son, Chris, was born – that when they became parents she would leave her retail job for a few years. Brian, a computer specialist, would support them single-handedly on his $35,000 annual earnings. So from the beginning the Arnolds lived on his salary alone, investing hers in a bank savings program and in occasional large-ticket purchases.

"My salary covered most of the down payment on our home, our car, all of our appliances, and much of our furniture," Kay says. "We have enough left over so that we have $18,000 earning interest in the bank. We occasionally tap these savings for emergencies – like when we had some heavy car repair bills last year – and once in a while for a luxury like a babysitter or an anniversary dinner out.

"Sure, the couch will wear out, and we'll need to replace the car someday," she adds, "but these are far enough down the pike that we can continue living on Brian's salary for the next few years. We plan to have another child within a year or so, and I hope to stay at home full-time until that child goes to school."

The Arnolds are typical of "planned sequencers" who never live day-to-day on two salaries and who make their major purchases before the first child is born. Such couples a) make it a point to draw all daily living expenses from the husband's salary from the beginning, b) use the wife's salary only for large one-time purchases, and c) save the remainder of the wife's salary, investing it in an interest-producing savings account or growth fund.

The most critical facet of this kind of planning is that if the couple is buying a home, monthly payments and taxes necessary to carry it must come from the husband's income alone. Otherwise, the couple can fall into a two-income dependency trap, as did Jim and Ruth Willmar. Although they had always assumed that when they became parents Ruth would leave her position as a nursing supervisor to be at home, it didn't work out as smoothly as they had hoped.

"Our big mistake was in buying a home we loved but for which we needed two salaries to meet monthly payments," says Ruth. Two months before the birth of their daughter Sara, Ruth left her job as planned and the couple began to live on Jim's clinical psychologist salary. But they just couldn't afford it: "The house payments were several hundred dollars a month too high for us. So after eight months I put Sara in home day care and went back to work. But I was miserable."

Within a few weeks, the Willmars saw that their choice was crystal clear: They either could have the home they loved empty all day, while both worked to pay for it, or Ruth could be home raising the child they loved – but in a different home.

"Once that choice became really clear," Ruth says, "we sold the house and moved to a much smaller one in a far less attractive neighborhood. But I love being home with Sara. I'm pregnant again and can truly say that we have no regrets about our decision. Someday, when our family is complete and the children are in school, I'll return to work again, and we may be able to afford a larger, nicer house. But it can wait; Sara will only be small once."

Unlike the Arnolds, who thoroughly planned for sequencing before their first child was born, the Willmars embraced sequencing in theory but failed to reckon with economic reality. Confronted with the conflict between keeping their house and Ruth's being home, they quickly found it no contest. Ruth's "We couldn't afford it" turned into "We found a way to afford the choice we wanted to make." The main reason their decision to sell the house was relatively easy is that they were committed to sequencing from the start – long before they even knew baby Sara.

Unplanned Sequencing

In contrast to the Arnolds and Willmars, many couples do not make a sequencing decision prior to the birth of their first child. Rather, they assume that their children will be in the care of others while they both work. Only after the birth of a child do their priorities change.

"How could I have known in advance that I'd love a helpless, incontinent, dribbling, burping, screaming little bundle of humanity more than my law practice?" laughs Joan Bomberg, who after five years on a Boston law partnership track left her firm to stay at home with her son, Matthew.

"This has not been an easy choice," says Joan. "Not only has it meant that I delay partnership by the number of years I am away from the office, but it has also made us restructure our financial expectations. And while nobody will cry for us that we had to drop to $80,000 from a joint income over $150,000, in the East Coast professions that is quite a comment on our values."

For the Bombergs that choice meant changing their lifestyle and their future expectations. "We've forgotten our plans for the new home we were going to build soon. Our 'starter' house will do just fine for a long time," Joan says. "We've also given up vacations abroad and fancy restaurant dinners on Saturday nights. Now we have friends over informally or go to inexpensive museum exhibits with them. We no longer expect that our children will attend private school or have private lessons when they are young. I don't plan to resume working for six or eight years, and until then all of these things are in the luxury category, on hold."

The Bombergs were surprised to find an unexpected financial upside to Joan's sequencing. "I never realized how much it cost me to work," Joan says. "All of a sudden, a number of expenses literally vanished with my job. For instance, now I am the nanny instead of paying somebody else to care for Matt. I've traded in designer suits for sweat suits. I do my own hair and nails. I've no daily transportation, parking, or lunch expenses. I've time to grocery shop with care rather than buy what's quickest, and I do the weekday cooking rather than bring takeout home for dinner."

When Bomberg resigned her $75,000 salary, she didn't in fact give up $75,000 in annual income. It was closer to $25,000. Nearly one-third of her gross earnings went for income taxes. After that, $12,000 went for child care; her "professional image" – wardrobe and beauty shop expenses plus transportation and lunches – totaled close to $10,000. She feels she easily saves $5,000 a year on food, since she shops more carefully and prepares meals rather than relies on expensive convenience foods, takeout, and restaurant dinners. So actually, her family has lost $25,000, not $75,000.

Andrea and Paul Lewis of Cleveland made a similar decision, but from another part of the economic continuum. Paul works as a machinist and earns about $20,000. Andrea, who left a $12,000 receptionist job following the birth of her second child this year, says, "I'd always expected to work straight through, just taking time for maternity leave. But I missed my two babies so much I just had to be with them. I've worked for pay since I was fifteen years old, and I will for the rest of my life. But right now, caring for my babies is work of a different sort and a lot harder than sitting and answering the phone all day."

While Andrea has encountered social stigma because of her choice, she maintains that she is doing more for society by raising her children herself than by leaving them in day care with providers and children who might not have the same strong values: "A good beginning is everything; I want to teach my children right and wrong and shower them with love and kisses while they're little."

The Lewises' decision was not without its price: they gave up their two-bedroom apartment for a smaller flat. Paul and Andrea sleep in the bedroom and have divided the living room into a sleeping area for the children and a family space with a couch and television set. The Lewises also sold their car, so they either walk or rely on public transportation.

Clothing costs are held to a minimum. "My cousins have older kids, and they always send me whatever theirs have outgrown," Andrea says. "I grocery shop on specials and cook healthy food for us – lots of beans, rice, and fruits and vegetables in season. So we are eating, we have a roof above us, and we have health benefits through Paul's work. Being without medical insurance was my greatest fear about leaving my job, but he pays extra for us and we're all signed on to his.

"We can't afford to pay babysitters, so we trade off babysitting with friends. They have a bigger apartment, so one weekend the four of us go over there on Saturday and take care of their kids while they go out, and the next week we bring the kids to them and we go out. It's something to look forward to. In between, our entertainment consists of watching television and sometimes a ninety-nine-cent video rental."

The financial loss to Andrea's family when she left her job was not her whole salary but rather about forty percent of it. From $12,000, her after-tax net was $9,200. Day care costs for both children came to more than $2,700 a year, and Andrea's clothes, transportation, and lunches totaled about $1,000, leaving roughly $5,500 to compensate for. The Lewises did it by making the major lifestyle changes Andrea describes above.

A Values Decision

Although the Bombergs and Lewises are at very different income levels, they share the major economic problems of unplanned sequencing with each other and with many thousands of similarly placed families. Since they didn't plan in advance, both couples had to cut back financially when they went from two paychecks to one. In so doing, they found that a number of expenses related to the woman's work vanished, so they did not in fact lose a whole paycheck – they had never had it.

Nevertheless, both families "lost" a significant proportion of their pay and had to create ways to compensate for that loss. In the Bombergs' case, the lost income was about $25,000; with the Lewises, it was nearly $5,500. Each couple found that lodging was affected. The Bombergs saw that moving to larger quarters would be an impossibility on their reduced income; the Lewises had to move to a smaller apartment. Each woman shopped and cooked more economically once the time crunch of full-time work was removed. Both developed new, less expensive means of entertainment, and both found ways to cut down on clothing expenses.

Whatever the loss of income, deciding to sequence when a couple has become dependent upon both incomes is always difficult and cannot be done overnight. Both partners must analyze their total economic picture calmly and thoroughly to see where they can make changes.

This financial analysis entails 1) listing all present income and expenses on the two salaries, 2) listing all projected expenses on one salary, 3) determining by how much the expense column exceeds the income column, and 4) deciding what kinds of lifestyle changes need to be made to cut projected expenses to meet income. This is the most difficult step and the one on which partners most often disagree. Arriving at a plan acceptable to both can take many hours of discussion and debate.

The experiences of the Arnolds and Willmars (who had long planned to sequence) and the Bombergs and Lewises (for whom this lifestyle change was unexpected) all demonstrate that sequencing is a values decision. This is not to say that sequencing is an appropriate choice for all married women, but rather that no woman who wants to sequence should conclude it is financially impossible before she and her husband have examined their finances and values that underlie the allocation of those resources.

Couples often find, as did the Bombergs and Lewises, that child care and other work-related expenses are much higher than they had realized. They see that after deducting taxes and expenses from the wife's salary, the amount of paycheck forgone if she leaves her work isn't nearly as much as they'd feared. They may find, as did the Willmars and Lewises, who moved to smaller quarters, that the decision of whether or not the mother can afford to be at home turns on where the home is.

To date, sequencing is an option exercised most frequently by married mothers. However, a small but growing number of fathers are electing to sequence while their wives work outside home. In a few years, as more men do, and as more employees view sequencing leave, part-time work, telecommuting, and more flexible work options as matters of course, we may see two-sequencer families. In these situations mothers and fathers may each, at different points in their families' lives, leave work for a period of years to focus their energies on raising their children. And if that happens, we may see not only stronger, more secure families, but persons less burned out from, and more productive in, their total work lives.♥

Arlene Rossen Cardozo has her Ph.D. in Mass Communication and teaches Mass Communication at the University of Minnesota. She is the author of Sequencing, *(Collier/MacMillan 1989), as well as three other books and numerous articles.*

This article originally appeared in the September 1990 issue, and is reprinted with permission from The World And I, *a publication of* The Washington Times Corporation, © *1990.*

Enterprising Woman
by Karen Zwolenski

Ed. note: All figures in this article are in 1986 dollars.

When I tearfully announced to my husband that I just didn't think I could leave our baby and resume my teaching job, his face paled. I'd always intended to continue fulltime work after the baby was born. I was sure that I could never "just be a mother at home." Ha! Little did I realize the immensity of the job of "just" staying home. Nor did I realize the incredible bond I would have with my daughter. I wanted to be with her during the days. I didn't want to miss a thing. My husband regained his composure and calmly said: "If that is what would make you happy, then do it. We'll find a way to manage." I'll never forget it. We discussed our finances and made the idea a reality. We were scared. Was it possible to live on $18,000 a year?

An income cut is frightening, but I reminded myself that I'd be saving money by staying home. How? By saving at least $400 per month in expenses.

My husband and I figured we could save on the following:

1. Child care for one child: $300 and up per month. Nanny care is more expensive; one acquaintance paid $800 per month.

2. Clothes (shoes, panty hose, purses, uniforms, blouses, skirts, suits): $50 per month.

3. Lunch/coffee: $50 per month ($2.50 per day).

4. Transportation (gas, insurance, maintenance): variable.

All costs vary, depending on the area in which one lives.

It helped us to rethink our approach to dealing with the loss of one income. In doing so, we listed ways in which we could save money. We realized that many of these ideas were actually "money makers." These ideas will show that it's possible to reorganize family expenditures. Reducing costs in one area frees income for another area.

Consider the following "enterprising activities" as a starting point for an at-home financial management job. It includes both my experiences and those of **Welcome Home** readers.

Infant Care

• BREASTFEED. It's nutritional and inexpensive. Breastfed babies have fewer infections, allergies, and illnesses, and that means fewer doctor visits, medical bills, and prescriptions. The expense of formula and bottles, at least $50 a month, can be eliminated.

• CLOTH DIAPERS. Disposable diapers and commercial wipes cost $40 to $60 per month. With more than one child, the expenditure is spread out, making it an even greater savings. Later, the old diapers make soft cloths for cleaning and dusting.

• BABY FOOD. A small food grinder is inexpensive and sometimes a blender works just as well. Use this to prepare nutritional baby food by using ingredients from family meals. Save time and prepare food for a week or two at a time. Many good books are available on this subject.

• EQUIPMENT AND CLOTHING. Stores and advertisers try to convince us otherwise, but babies need far less equipment, toys, and clothing than most people think.

One acquaintance didn't have to pinch pennies, but forever practical, she and her husband decided against buying baby furniture. "Friends told us most baby furniture was impractical in the long run, so instead we bought inexpensive, colorful stacked bins that slide like drawers and used these for storing clothing. We used the crib my husband and his siblings used. When our children outgrew the crib, we bought them beds, but we didn't buy furniture until they were five years old. Today our children use the bins for their toys."

Car seats, strollers, high chairs, and the like aren't as easily substituted. (Never substitute a bargain for safety.)

Try shopping for these items (or for furniture) at consignment stores, yard sales, and community white elephant sales, as they offer outstanding values often in excellent condition.

Food

• PLANNING MENUS. By planning menus before shopping, I'm usually able to take better advantage of sales and the low cost of seasonal products when they are most available.

• CLIPPING COUPONS. Mothers have successfully reduced their food budget with this method. Books and articles are available on this topic. I cut out the coupons I think I will use, but only those that can be applied to products that fit into my meal plan and budget. I only cut out coupons that are worth 20 cents or more and keep them in a separate coupon holder in my purse. It's a quick and easy way to make some money. I use about $2-3 worth per week, $104-156 a year!

• CHANGING DIETS. We've tightened our belts literally and figuratively. How? Simply by eating less animal protein and more grains and legumes, we've saved money and cut back on fat and cholesterol.

• REDUCING EXPENDITURES. The "budget busters" of any shopping list are convenience foods, snack and dessert foods, items packaged in small amounts, and impulse purchases. My husband and I are developing a whole new set of eating habits as well as shopping habits.

• DISCOVERING NEW MARKETS. Local markets may not offer the best prices. When feasible, I shop at discount stores, food co-ops, wholesale outlets, local farms, and markets that offer lower prices. Traveling time may increase and it may not be convenient, but I've noticed the difference at the cash register. One may be able to save up to $100 a month.

• GARDENING. This turned out to be a larger option than I realized. No backyard? No shovels? No problem! A friend with an apartment grows produce in containers on a small porch. Relaxation and satisfaction are additional benefits. Why not plant some flowering seeds or bulbs for inexpensive fresh bouquets?

Freezing or canning your produce will allow you an out-of-season supply. Sweet corn, peas, cooked squash, and pumpkin all can be frozen. Strawberries and raspberries can be frozen or made into jam. Tomatoes can be canned whole or made into spaghetti sauce. Potatoes, onions, or carrots can be stored by hanging them in net bags in your cool basement or garage.

Transportation

• Owning and maintaining a car is expensive. Many husbands are able to commute by public transportation. Purchasing quality used cars is not difficult and can save money not only in the purchase price but in taxes and insurance as well.

• Planning errands and recreation needs can save gasoline costs.

Entertainment

This is the area of the family budget that is slashed most drastically when a family reduces its income. It also is one of the areas that offers the opportunity to be most creative. Think twice before dining out. If dining out, drink water instead of soft drinks. On weekends dine out for lunch instead of dinner, since lunch prices generally are lower. For those who own a VCR, many libraries offer video rentals free or for a nominal fee. It's much less than going to a theater. You will find many ways to cut corners.

A common problem for parents of younger children is finding time for themselves. Babysitters are the answer but their cost is considerable, even for a night out. There is another way! Swap child care with friends. A friend and I take turns every other week caring for each other's child so as to have some time with our spouses.

Motherhood takes perseverance, energy, flexibility, and commitment. Managing your financial enterprise at home will use all of these resources. The above list is not comprehensive but an outline for your own plan and efforts. Other mothers will be your greatest source for more ideas. Remember that you are not alone in meeting the challenges of being an enterprising woman. ♥ © 1988

Karen Zwolenski writes from her home in Northfield, Minnesota. She is the mother of Megan (five) and Lauren (three). Karen is the author of "Letting Dad Get Involved" in this book.

Kitchen Dancing

by Susan Rockwell

The time? Midnight.
My gown? A fuzzy robe.
The music? A quiet radio.
The lighting? Dim glow of the digital clock.
My partner? A little bald man (only three months old).

We swing and sway in each other's arms as the night ticks by, oblivious to the rest of the world. My restless partner melts into my chest and we become one...again. Tonight I dream of a night on the town. Someday, my dreams will be of kitchen dancing.♥ © 1991

Susan Rockwell, mom of Lisa (five) and Russell (two) lives in Grandville, Michigan. She says, "My son continued to get me up several times a night until he turned two. But now he sleeps through the night. I made it! Just thought other mothers with restless sleepers might like to know there is an end to it!"

Singing With Joy

by Wendy Underhill

"Do you talk to your baby?" Dr. Penny Thron-Weber asked a teenager who came in for a checkup with her three-month-old baby to a clinic in Denver. "No, I wouldn't know what to say," the young mother replied. The doctor explained the importance of verbal communication with babies, saying it has to start long before the little ones are able to respond in kind. Babies learn the rhythms of communication and get a chance to develop language from their attempts to repeat what is said. Mostly, though, words represent love to a baby.

"Do you sing to the baby?" the doctor asked. "Sometimes singing is easier for a new mother, if she feels uncomfortable just talking."

"No, I don't know any songs that are good for a baby," the mother responded.

Dr. Thron-Weber advised that "any song would do. It doesn't have to be a lullaby or other 'baby' song. Why not try the songs from the Top Forty?"

When the young mother came back for her next visit, she reported feeling a stronger warmth for her child, and the baby looked brighter and more involved. These changes might have occurred regardless of the song, but the musical communication almost certainly helped.

When my first child, Vivian, came, I found myself in the same boat as the young mother at the clinic. I didn't know what to say to my baby! It is a myth that mothers instinctively know what to do and say to a baby; child care does not always come naturally. It didn't for me, as it didn't for the teenage mom at the clinic. So I took Dr. Thron-Weber's advice.

I started with a tape of lullabies and sang along with them. Then I tried recordings of songs from *South Pacific, West Side Story*, and other Broadway shows. Pretty soon, I knew the words to all these songs and didn't need the records any more.

I sang while changing diapers, nursing, and cuddling. I sang as I wandered about the house comforting little Vivi, and I sang when we went for walks or errands. A strange thing happened, though. The songs changed! The new lyrics that popped out of my mouth tended to have words like "love" and "baby" and "Vivi" instead of the standard ones.

My voice is nothing special; I can't always carry a tune. Fortunately, a trained voice isn't important when you are singing to babies. My husband sings Bach chorales and Brahms lieder in concert; he didn't sing those songs – or anything else – to our daughter at first. After hearing the nonsense songs I came up with, he

started making up his own. Anyone can do it, and babies love it.

I may be as "corny as Kansas in August," as the song says, but I'm a believer in the power of song now. ♥ © 1990

Wendy Underhill, mother of Vivian (nearly three) and Audrey (one), writes from her home in Boulder, Colorado. She is a freelance writer in her "spare" time, which she defines as "time when I otherwise would be cleaning or cooking."

Anything Worth Doing

by Linda Bricker

For years, people have told me: "Anything worth doing is worth doing well." "Don't start something you can't finish." I disagree. If I wait until I have time or money to "do things right," they may not get done at all. So I am willing to settle for doing parts of things that are worth doing.

When the whole house is in chaos and we must leave for swimming lessons in half an hour, I can't clean up the whole mess, but I can do the dishes and pick up some of the clutter – and feel much better about it. When my son is overwhelmed by his room full of dirty clothes, books, and baseball cards, I can have him pick up one or two of these things. It's an improvement, and he feels much better accomplishing something. We might even be inspired to finish the job later, since it's not as bad as it was.

When my three children want to spark up a trip to town with lunch out somewhere, but the budget won't stretch, we still can picnic in the park and stop for an ice cream cone on the way home.

Even a letter to a friend can be condensed, and the receiver will love your five-minute note just because you thought of her. I know; I have received many of them. Those short messages are a real boost, whether the day is crazy or dull.

If you can't do something right, it is better to do it halfway with a cheerful attitude than to be depressed over leaving it undone. Happy halfways! ♥ © 1991

Linda Bricker lives on a farm in Albany, Oregon. Her children now are sixteen, thirteen, and ten years old. In addition to her farm work, she now has a job in an office with a flex-time policy so she can be with her children for special events and when they are sick. She writes, "Thank goodness I was able to be there at least until our youngest was ten. They still require large doses of nurturing."

Resisting Peer Pressure: Not Just For Kids

by Cornelia Odom

One of the things that puts babies in a class by themselves is that, unlike everyone else, they don't know yet that they have any peers, much less allow their tastes to be dictated by them. I've never seen a baby yet who was trying to earn, by action or appearance, the approval of another baby. I've seen friendly overtures on the part of one baby toward another, and I've seen the watchful scrutiny that babies give to everything, especially to other babies and children. But I've yet to witness a baby who truly was out to impress one of his peers. When you see an unassuming baby, it's startling to realize that all too soon his self-consciousness will come to the fore, and that the days inevitably are approaching when more and more of his decisions and preferences will be made with reference to those of his agemates.

It's understandable to view this natural progression with ambivalence. We know all too well that susceptibility to peer pressure in the teen years begets many evils – reckless driving, acts of vandalism, teenage pregnancy, drug dependency. Once we become parents ourselves, we may shudder at the memory of choices we made in our youth, the foolish chances we took. We begin to look askance at the current youth culture.

We want to raise kids who are able to resist self-destructive impulses and self-degrading attempts to win acceptance. But the attitudes our kids will have toward their peers don't arise abruptly with the onset of puberty. The foundations of a healthy understanding of the relationship between self and peers are laid by parents, beginning in infancy.

Much has been written about the crucial need of children to develop a sense of self-esteem which will protect them from being unduly swayed by the whims of the crowd. Parents need to tell their children, often and by word and deed, that they are loved unconditionally, that they are valued as individuals, and that they are welcomed and accepted members of the family. As children grow, parents can begin to encourage them to form and defend their own opinions, and they can listen respectfully to their children's expressions of their tastes. In order to employ these practices successfully, however, parents need to reflect on their own desire for approval and acceptance from their own peers and from the culture at large.

We all hope that our kids will be well-adjusted, liked by others, and able to succeed in the world. But to the degree that we are anxious and dubious about this, to the degree that our own self-esteem depends on how well our kids "fit in," we may find ourselves pressuring them to be more like other kids.

As you shop for your baby or child, do you wonder why you are drawn to the designer clothing racks, despite the presence nearby of perfectly serviceable, lower-priced choices? When your friends discuss preschool possibilities for their children, are you filled with a vague anxiety and a sense of competitiveness, even though you haven't yet decided whether preschool is right for your child at all? Have you ever wondered at the sheer variety of lessons available for infants and children (gym, swim, art, dance, music...) and asked yourself how a parent possibly can discern whether his young child possesses any interest, aptitude, or readiness for these activities?

The amount of decision-making that raising kids calls into play makes it tempting just to do what everyone else seems to be doing. But there is a catch: when we make choices for our kids based largely on the choices of our peers, we are setting up our children to use the same criteria when the time comes for them to make their own choices. If parents want to instill in their children an ability to resist peer pressure, we'll have to begin by joining the struggle to resist it ourselves. Sometimes it just takes an offhand remark or two to show us where we're vulnerable.

When I was pregnant with my first child, it really distressed me that I was unable to afford the deluxe, coordinated nursery ensembles that so many of my friends had. I wanted the cute crib sets, too, with the matching bumpers, quilt, and dust ruffle. I wanted to be choosing wallpaper and curtains. My image of what an expectant mother should be doing included the task (unaffordable for me) of "decorating the nursery."

As my due date approached, I remember complaining fretfully to a friend that I "didn't have the nursery ready." "Oh, dear!" he exclaimed. "I hear babies really get upset about that."

It was just what I wanted to hear and what, as my children grow, I continue to need to hear, over and over again. It's hard in our society to disentangle our own motives and desires from what we see our peers doing and having. It takes practice to discern the differences between what our kids really need from us and what's just for show. Two common areas in which parents let peer pressure guide their choices for their children are clothing and extracurricular activities. In a department store I overheard a mother who was trying to strike a bargain with her preschooler. The child was tired and uninterested, the mother not yet ready to call it a day. In an effort to enlist her daughter's cooperation, the mother exclaimed, "Oh, look at this pretty dress! Wouldn't you like to try this one on? It's just like Amy's!" A child at the end of such an exchange cannot help but receive a not-very-subtle message – that looking pretty involves looking like someone else. Small wonder that many children reach their teens and feel an absolute compulsion to dress like their peers. Another time I found myself listening to a mother describing her daughter's involvement on the local swim team. "Does Jamie enjoy swimming?" I politely inquired, expecting to receive an affirmative answer. A blank look crossed the face of Jamie's mother. "I don't know if she enjoys it or not," she finally replied in a what's-that-got-to-do-with-it tone of voice. "All of her friends are on the team."

I don't quote these remarks to be critical of other mothers. Making choices for children while encouraging their unique personalities to emerge is quite a job! We've all said worse things than these in moments of frustration. My point is that, more often than we care to admit, it is the parent rather than the child who gives voice to the old refrain, "All of the kids are doing it!"

To be sure, we don't often begin with these words. At first we're overtaken with delight at the uniqueness of our new babies, firmly convinced that each one is special. We're thrilled that there's no other baby in the world quite like our baby. But new motherhood is also a time of doubt and uncertainty, a new role for which we often haven't been very well-prepared. There was a time when I simply couldn't help comparing my child's development with that of other babies her age. It wasn't so much that I felt she had to be the first and the best; I just wanted that blessed assurance that she was normal.

And so I compared notes with other parents. Who's sleeping through the night? Who's eating solid food, who's crawling, who's got teeth? I gleaned a lot of invaluable information from these exchanges. I'd recommend them to any new mother, with a caveat: Beware of how this approach to childrearing can evolve! Soon the question becomes: Who's going to nursery school and where? Who's taking gym lessons? Who's started violin?

I am not advocating that we deliberately distance ourselves from our friends and neighbors. Parents can learn a lot from each other. The important thing is simply for parents to realize that the pressure they feel to raise kids in the acceptable mode may well have a trickle-down effect. When you make a decision for your child, take an extra minute to examine your motives. Resist the temptation to nudge your child into an activity primarily because the other kids his age are doing it. Try not to insist to strenuously that he dress in a manner which upholc your image as the parent of a with-it kid. Don't use y children to try to impress anyone, not even yourse

As with so many childrearing principles, it's not as easy as it sounds. Not all kids hear a different drummer. It isn't necessarily true that if you encourage your child to be his own person, he'll never yearn to run with the pack. But since so much else in our society directs us toward conformity, can't we at least assure our children that we value how unique each of them really and mysteriously is? Can't we encourage that uniqueness to take root and blossom by paying close attention to each child's interests and talents and by allowing him to travel his own path, whatever it may be? Can we give our children now, while they still are young, the assurance that we'll love them in the unknowable future, even if it turns out that they aren't as popular or successful as the neighbor's kids, even if they never take us up on all we've got planned for them?

It's never too soon to start conveying this message. Your baby doesn't care what the other babies are wearing. He isn't worried about what the other babies think of him, or about what their mothers think of him either, for that matter. He's taking all of his cues from you. As he grows and his childhood unfolds, it's your acceptance and approval he craves, and it's your values he's assimilating. His self-esteem and his ability to withstand peer pressure in adolescence and into adulthood depend – to a significant degree – upon the lessons you are teaching him now.♥ © 1991

Cornelia Odom is the mother of two children, ages eight and six. She lives in Washington, D.C., and enjoys writing, walking, and reading historical fiction. She homeschools her children and edits a monthly newsletter for homeschooling families. Since 1989, she has been writing and editing for **Welcome Home**.

Cooped Up?
Join A Co-op!

by Joanne Bruun

Imagine a rendezvous for lunch with your husband. Imagine celebrating a friend's birthday with relaxed conversation around a table set with china and fresh flowers. Imagine heading for a good sale at the mall or spending several quiet hours at home alone.

Imagine no more. Join or start a babysitting co-op and these "lost" freedoms of your b.c.(before children) years will be yours again. Here's how.

Size It Up. You need about twenty families, but you can start with a dozen and work up. I knew a co-op with sixty families but it's hard for members to know one another in a group that large. A co-op with twenty families enables you to find playmates for your children even at those busy times when moms are helping with school holiday parties.

When I started my co-op, we limped along with about six members for a year. It seemed everyone I knew thought being in a co-op meant enduring endless hours of sitting. My experience in co-ops in two states has been that it actually means two to three sits a month. My co-op took off when I convinced a good friend to join who lives in a neighborhood with a lot of young families. When the other moms saw how great it was, the co-op filled up. We have since expanded to thirty families to accommodate some of those on the waiting list.

Keep It Close. You don't want to spend precious co-op time driving, so confine your co-op to your immediate area, if possible. My co-op comprises five developments, but we are all within a two-mile radius.

Here's The Ticket. Time is not money in the babysitting co-op. Time is tickets. In my co-op we use popsicle sticks with "co-op" stamped on them. Some groups use index cards. Any medium of exchange that is durable will do. We start off each new member with thirty sticks.

Pay As You Go. Each ticket, card, popsicle stick, or whatever currency you use is worth one half-hour of sitting time. So if you leave your child for one hour, you pay two sticks when you pick up your child. If you leave two children, you pay time and a half, that is, three sticks an hour. Three children is double time, or four sticks an hour. I keep my sticks in the glove compartment.

Co-op Roster Spells Relief. Your co-op roster is better than the Yellow Pages. It should contain the following information: mother's name and phone number, address, husband's name and work phone, pediatrician's name and number, the children's names, dates of birth, and allergies, and any times you are not available to sit, such as "No T, Th a.m."

Simple Does It. The presidency of the co-op rotates alphabetically every three months. At the end of her term, the president holds a co-op meeting in her home and the former president brings a refreshment. In this way the president only has to straighten her living room to prepare for the meeting. Because this is a pay-as-you-go co-op, no bookkeeper or secretary is necessary.

Every co-op establishes its own rules. Some co-ops use signed medical releases in the event of an emergency. Seek advice in your area. Most co-ops accept new members on the recommendation of current members. Make guidelines you feel comfortable with but keep them simple.

The Golden Rule You Can Co-op By. The Golden Rule of the co-op is this:

a) When you are out of tickets, you can't use the co-op, and

b) When you have the maximum number of tickets (in my co-op we set the number at sixty), you can't accept sits. This keeps the tickets in circulation and prevents one nice mom who can't say no from doing too much sitting.

Mom's Night Out. Four times a year, the co-op meets to see how things are going, to iron out any problems, to introduce new members, and to update the roster. Basically, it's a good excuse to get together and chat. My co-op combines its December meeting with a cookie exchange. Occasionally, we have used a meeting to discuss a topic, such as ideas for the long hot summer.

Sit By Starlight. Some co-ops are also used for evening sits. Women who use co-ops in the evening tell me that they feel more comfortable leaving their children with an adult. Others say they can't afford teenage sitters and this allows them to get out more often with their husbands. Unlike daytime sits which are done in your home, at night you travel to the child's home. Moms say this is a wonderful way to read, write letters, sew, or just relax in a way they wouldn't if they were home.

My co-op puts an E for evening next to the parent's names who are available for night sits.

Way To Go, Mama. The best way to be used by the co-op is to use the co-op. This is especially true if you are new, as people are hesitant to call new members. However, once you have used a few moms, they will be more likely to call you. Now is **not** the time to sit waiting for your phone to ring. When I moved to Texas, I sat down with the co-op roster and circled the names of women with children the ages of mine. Then I invited these families, one at a time, to visit. While the kids played, the mom and I got to know one another over coffee. I made friends, so did the kids, and when I needed to go out, I knew whom to call.

At my birthday party this year, a friend asked each person to tell how they had met me. We had a good laugh when one mom after another said I had invited them to join the co-op and described how that invitation had changed their lives.

I'd like to tell you what a warm moment that was and how much these women mean to me, but I have to go. I am sitting for my friend Rosemary today so she can go on a field trip with her son. Rosemary is looking forward to "introducing the second graders to the naked ladies at the National Gallery of Art." Don't be cooped up. Join a co-op!♥ © 1990

For ten years, from Texas to Maryland, Joanne Bruun has enjoyed the friendships and free time that come with babysitting co-ops. She is a long-time senior editor of **Welcome Home**. *Joanne, her husband Bob, and sons Andrew (sixteen), Matthew (fifteen), Dan (thirteen), and daughter Suzanne (eight), reside in Ellicott City, Maryland.*

A Mother's Prayer

*There are a thousand interruptions
in my day, Lord —
All my household jobs
in ten steps to finish!
Little hands and little feet
wanting to help and needing to learn.*

*When I had a career,
I liked to do things very fast and very well,
while in this new job,
to do them well eliminates doing them fast.*

*My speech is repetitive:
Don't pull the cat's tail.
Drink your milk slowly
out of the big girl's cup.
Walk carefully downstairs.
A thousand times I want to shout,
"Hurry up!" but I stop,
and take a deep breath,
and guide this little person.*

*Today I hear her talking to her dolls....
"Walk slow," she says.
"Be careful," she says.
"Watch Mommy," she says.
"You're precious," she says.*

*And I know that all of those interruptions
weren't really interruptions at all.
They were opportunities.*

Kristy Fickert

Networks For Mothers

*by Barbara Jean Comstock
and Pamela M. Goresh*

There was a time when a mother at home could walk outside and meet her neighbors. Neighbors with children for her children to play with, neighbors to join for a cup of coffee and a discussion of the daily joys and frustrations of motherhood. Her extended family may have lived close by, providing support for her.

Life isn't that simple today. The urban, suburban, and rural landscapes have been altered. Many mothers wonder if they will ever find friends for themselves or for their children. And what about answers for all those questions they have about their babies? Where can they find comfort for the flood of new emotions no one told them they'd be feeling? What's a mother to do?

For mothers who previously enjoyed busy work, school, and social lives, the prospect of being at home with their young children may appear to be restrictive and unchallenging. However, today's mothers at home are overcoming their possible isolation by joining or creating a variety of support groups and networks. In turn, these new types of communities are assisting mothers to develop confidence in their roles as well as to explore new opportunities for personal growth and accomplishment.

The following list of resources is a starting point for finding or creating a group to meet your unique needs. Often, becoming involved is as easy as posting a few signs or making a few phone calls. Probably the most important thing to remember as you begin this search is that you are not alone! As you begin to approach mothers at home, you will find others with common interests, fears, hopes, and a need to come together to support each other.

Support Groups And Centers

Many national support group organizations help women make the adjustment to motherhood. Some are directed specifically at those mothers who choose to be at home to care for their children.

Other groups address specialized needs and interests, while at the same time providing overall support. For some mothers, the need or desire to begin a home-based business presents an opportunity to locate or develop a group or network which can support her both as a mother and as an entrepreneur.

The desire to remain in contact with her previous career may be the reason for a mother to start a mothers support group through a local professional association. In Washington, D.C., the Women's Bar Association recently began such a group by placing a notice in the local bar association monthly publication. Called "Lawyers At Home Forum," it provides support and advocacy for attorneys who are at home or those who work parttime.

The group has over one hundred forty members in its first year of operation.

Finally, volunteer activities may offer opportunities for mothers with young children to work together in support of common interests and values, thereby combining the satisfaction of service and community participation along with mother support. The following organizations offer a variety of support and information:

THE FAMILY RESOURCE COALITION
200 South Michigan Avenue
Suite 1520
Chicago IL 60604-2404
(312) 341-0900

The coalition provides a vast amount of information on how to start or find parents' groups. By calling or writing, you can get a list of the existing groups in your area as well as a packet of information on how to start a group. The coalition recommends first checking the phone book under "Family, Child, or Children" for agencies that provide services for families. The early childhood education department of a local college might be able to tell you where to find parent education programs and support groups. Hospitals are another source of parent education/support programs. Although hospital classes may be geared primarily toward parents of newborns, such classes may be a means for new mothers to start meeting other mothers.

Local churches, the YMCA, the YWCA, and the local chapter of the Childbirth and Parent Education Association also may provide local support activities or suggestions for finding them.

MOMS CLUB
814 Moffat Circle
Simi Valley CA 93065
(805) 526-2725

The MOMS (Moms Offering Moms Support) Club with over fifty groups nationwide provides information on how to start and manage a support group for at-home mothers in your area. Individual groups typically offer monthly meetings with speakers, playgroups, community service projects, instructional programs, babysitting co-ops, and other activities that reflect members' interests. Groups are non-denominational.

MOPS INTERNATIONAL
4175 Harlan Street
Wheat Ridge CO 80033
(303) 420-6100

MOPS' (Mothers Of Preschoolers) purpose is to help connect mothers; meetings follow the school calendar. While moms meet to share information, have small group time, and learn a craft, their children play nearby with supervision. MOPS has 470 local groups nationwide and offers charters to churches interested in starting groups.

HOME BY CHOICE
P.O. Box 103
Vienna VA 22183
(703) 281-6334

Home By Choice is a national Christian organization for mothers who choose to be at home. It provides practical help in starting a support group in your area or helping you to find one. It also offers a regular newsletter ($15.00 a year, bimonthly) to link the many Home By Choice groups and members.

FEMALE
P.O. Box 31
Elmhurst IL 60126
(708) 941-3553

FEMALE (Formerly Employed Mothers At The Leading Edge) is a support and advocacy group for women taking time out from paid employment to raise their children at home. There are over forty chapters nationally. A $20.00 membership includes a monthly newsletter. Local chapter startup materials and ongoing assistance are provided.

MOTHERING SEMINARS, INC.
P.O. Box 712
Columbia MD 21045
(301) 381-5195

This national nonprofit organization is for parents of children from birth to three. BYO Baby to a five-week seminar (held in homes, hospitals, or community centers) to meet other parents and to share laughs and cries and to gather information. Topics include: Coping With Change; Family Relationships; Development and Stimulation; Health, Safety, and Nutrition; and Reestablishing Intimacy as a Couple. There is a nominal fee. Write for a free listing of area seminars (twenty-five branches nationwide). Send $2 for a training packet if you are interested in becoming a consultant to provide these seminars for other parents.

NATIONAL ASSOCIATION OF MOTHERS' CENTERS
336 Fulton Avenue
Hempstead NY 11550
(800) 645-3828

The association provides nationwide information on how to locate or start a mothers' center. In addition, it has a list of existing centers.

The association was created to "provide a forum in which mothers and professionals work together to counteract the isolation mothers encounter, and to give recognition to the fact that they need a supportive environment in which to grow and develop as parents and individuals."

A mothers' center can be started with just two or three enthusiastic mothers willing to organize, find meeting space, and get the word out to other interested mothers. The Mothers' Center Development Project will provide an interested person with information on how to start a mothers' center in her area. Detailed instructions along with a manual on ways to generate interest in such a program are included.

KIDS FIRST
Lake View Postal Outlet
P.O. Box 36032
6449 Crowchild Trail S.W.
Calgary, Alberta T3E 7C6
(403) 289-1440

KIDS FIRST is a Canadian nonprofit organization concerned with the care and well-being of children. It provides parent support groups with over eighteen chapters in five provinces. It is also a child care policy advocate group, whose purpose is to protect the right and choice of parents to raise their children in a home setting. A one-year membership is $15.00 Canadian funds and includes a regular newsletter.

Special Interest/Needs Groups

Some groups address specialized needs and interests while at the same time providing overall support.

LA LECHE LEAGUE
INTERNATIONAL
9616 Minneapolis Avenue
Franklin Park IL 60131
(708) 455-7730

A non-sectarian, not-for-profit corporation, La Leche (Spanish for "the milk") offers support, encouragement, and information about breastfeeding. Founded thirty-five years ago by seven mothers, LLLI now has over three thousand groups in the U.S. and fifteen countries. LLLI offers a bimonthly magazine and a list of support groups in your area. It provides extensive training in many areas of child development, and special leadership training for its support group leaders.

CONNEXIONS
P.O. Box 1461
Manassas VA 22110
(703) 791-6264

CONNEXIONS is a quarterly networking newsletter for home-based entrepreneurial mothers. It offers timely information on beginning and managing a home-based business while rearing one's children. In addition, it encourages the development of local support groups for home business mothers. $14.95 a year.

Playgroups

For mothers interested in support groups on a smaller scale, a playgroup for preschool children or a babysitting co-op can provide an excellent way to obtain that much-needed contact with other mothers in similar situations. Julie Gilbert, who started a successful playgroup when her son was sixteen months old, says, "It's something you know will save your sanity...and you will be amazed how all the other mothers will help you out in starting a group because we're all in the same boat...we need other mothers to talk to and share our experiences with."

To start her playgroup, Julie posted several signs at local playgrounds and grocery stores. She also approached mothers with children who appeared close in age to her son. "At first I was looking for about ten mothers, but all you really need is three mothers and three kids and you have a playgroup," says Julie. In her group, a core of four mothers consistently kept up with the playgroup while others participated at various times over the years.

For a mother with a first child, the best type of playgroup probably would be one at which the mothers stay with their children. First-time mothers might find that they need time with other mothers as much as their children need a chance to meet playmates. For older children, a playgroup in which mothers rotate babysitting duties may prove more practical, especially if the mothers are not able to devote many hours to the playgroup. With either arrangement, it is best to start small to establish the best routine (schedule, time, snacks, activities) for those involved. Smaller groups can meet comfortably in homes. Larger groups may need more space, such as a community center, park, or place of worship.

Getting Started

With all these opportunities, it would appear to be easy to meet mothers at home. Often, however, it still can be a long road to finding the group that is just right for you. It can be like dating: You may have to spend time with different people in order to find the right match.

A good way to start is to think of your interests and then think of ways you might find friends who would share them. With this in mind, you are better prepared to start your search.

Keeping It Going

Joining or starting a group is only part of the story. The successful development and continuation of any support group depends on the effective communication and commitment of its members. Many of the groups listed in this article offer information to encourage good meeting management and group development. You also may check your local library for books or tapes about support group development. It may help to get the advice of someone with experience in leading groups. Your local hospital, YMCA, college, or place of worship all are likely to have someone who could help you with this aspect of support groups.

Big or small, all these groups can provide the crucial support mothers need to enable them to enjoy and grow in their challenging, worthwhile work.♥ © 1988

Barbara Jean Comstock, McLean, Virginia, is the mother of three children: Danny (eight), Peter (six), and Caity (three). She attended law school at night while a mother at home. Recently she has secured a flextime position on the Congressional staff of Rep. Frank Wolf, where she works on family and business issues. Pamela M. Goresh, a resident of Ellicott City, Maryland, is the mother of Samantha (ten) and Alexandra (seven). She enjoys reading, walking, and swimming. Pam works from her home as editor-in-chief of **Welcome Home.**

Special Resources

The following list of organizations is a starting place for finding information and support when faced with challenges or serious problems.

The American Self-Help Clearinghouse
St. Clare's-Riverside Medical Center
Pocono Road, Denville NJ 07834
(201-625-7101). This group provides current information about and referrals to seven hundred national self-help organizations and local clearinghouses; and to model one-of-a-kind self-help groups, or to individuals interested in beginning a group or national network. It also provides consultation on how to start a support group if one does not exist which addresses one's needs, and it publishes the annual *Self-Help Sourcebook.*

The American Academy Of Pediatrics
141 Northwest Point Boulevard, P.O. Box 927
Elk Grove Village IL 60009-0927
(708-228-5005). For booklets on any topic dealing with child or adolescent health and safety, send a self-addressed stamped envelope with your request for information on the specific topic and age group. On the envelope, state the topic you are requesting, then Dept. C, and the address.

RESOLVE, Inc.
1310 Broadway, Somerville MA 02144-1731
(617-623-0744). This national organization provides information, counseling, advocacy, support, and referral to people with problems of infertility.

Parent Care, Inc.
9041 Colgate Street, Indianapolis IN 46268-1210
(317-872-9913). The mission of Parent Care, Inc., is to offer information, direct referrals, and provide forums for discussion and services to families, parent support groups, and professionals concerned with infants who require intensive or special care at birth. Many services are available, including a quarterly newsletter, state networking, regional seminars, and an annual international conference.

National Organization For Rare Diseases/Disorders
P.O. Box 8923, New Fairfield CT 06812-1783
(800-999-6673). Acting as a clearinghouse on rare diseases and disorders, NORD helps families with similar disorders to network for mutual support. Call or write for an information packet and for support group referral.

National Organization of Mothers Of Twins Clubs Inc.
P.O. Box 23188, Albuquerque NM 87192-1188
(505-275-0955). NOMOTC provides support and information to parents of all multiples. It conducts research and education and disseminates it through its national network of local parent support groups. Call or write for a free brochure and referral to the nearest support group.

SHARE: Pregnancy and Infant Loss Support, Inc.
St. Joseph's Health Center
300 First Capitol Drive, St. Charles MO 63301
(314-947-5000). SHARE provides support and information to families experiencing miscarriage, stillbirth, perinatal death, and sudden infant death syndrome. The group has educational packets on a wide variety of topics available and it offers referrals to over two hundred and fifty support groups.

The Compassionate Friends, Inc.
National Headquarters
P.O. Box 3696, Oakbrook IL 60522-3696
(708-990-0010). This organization supports and aids parents and siblings in the positive resolution of the grief experience upon the death of their child (any age or reason for death) and to foster the physical and emotional health of the parents and siblings. Free brochures are available on a variety of topics. Referrals are made to six hundred forty chapters nationwide.

Unite, Inc., Grief Support
7600 Central Avenue, Philadelphia PA 19111-2499
(215-728-3777). This group provides written materials and information about local support groups to parents who have experienced the death of a baby during pregnancy and shortly after. It offers a bimonthly newsletter and acts as a clearinghouse of information for related groups and research.

SIDS (Sudden Infant Death Syndrome) Alliance
10500 Little Patuxent Parkway, Suite 420
Columbia MD 21044
(800-221-7437). The alliance will send a packet of information and make referrals to a local SIDS chapter. It also has other grief-related literature available.

Child Help U.S.A.
(800-422-4453). This group has a twenty-four-hour hotline for parents who are, or are concerned about becoming, abusive.

Parents Anonymous
(800-421-0353). Parents Anonymous has over one thousand self-help groups nationwide for parents who are, or are concerned about becoming, abusive to their children.

For help dealing with spouse abuse or other difficult situations, contact your local self-help clearinghouse, local helpline, or protective services organization.

Editor's note: for information about postpartum depression, see page 38. For resources on adoption, see page 74.

Growing In Unexpected Ways

A Mother's Vacation

by Robin Morris

It was Richard's first summer and my first vacation as a parent. The plan was to meet up with two other couples (who still were waiting to have children) at the beach for a week of R and R. We were heading to the very same beach that I had gone to as a child. My memories were rich, and my anticipation of the ocean air and late nights of wine and song was high.

Things went wrong from the start. I got a whopper of a cold, and then Richard caught it. I still was wearing my "baby fat," and no swimsuit could cover the evidence. Richard's fair skin precluded naps outdoors, and he was his normal fussy self indoors. And perhaps worst of all, the other two couples were ready for the time of their lives.

The first few days brought depression. The second few, downright anger and resentment. I got an hour of babysitting here and there, but the price was an expectation that I would feel everything was fine and dandy, an unspoken demand that I stop spoiling everyone's fun.

I couldn't explain how I was feeling, why I found there was no mental "time off" from Richard, even if there was a short physical separation. I could not explain how I mourned not being the child, the one taken care of instead of the one taking care. I could not express my inner fear that there might never be a childhood for me again. I could only cry at feeling trapped by parenthood.

Lost and lonely, my temper and tears flew alternately. My friends were concerned that I was not adjusting well to motherhood and wondered if I really loved my son. Some week at the beach.

When I returned home, now questioning myself as a good enough mother, I sought out the advice of other mothers. "You really thought you could have a vacation?" they asked, laughing. Soon I was laughing with them. I had survived my first real rite of passage into motherhood.♥

To Parent Is To Grow

by *Karolynn F. Coleman*

Before I became a mother, I had spent eight years as a fulltime clinical social worker specializing in family, adolescent, and child therapy. After my children arrived, I limited my professional work to a few hours of clinical work a week. I also began to read more extensively about child and adult development. My professional interest, coupled with firsthand parenting experience, motivated me to learn more about the ways that parenting can stimulate important growth and development in adults. I feel there is a need to describe the particular skills, attributes, and knowledge parents acquire as they tend to their children's development.

Researchers have paid very little attention to this subject for a number of reasons. Until recently, our theories of personality and human development have been primarily the products of men; results have been derived from studies of the lives of men. The researchers were perceiving matters through their own eyes on the basis of their own values and experiences. As a result, most of the literature on adult development focused on acts of individual achievement, usually in the marketplace. Even when more women performed social science research, there was scant interest in studying this subject; the reason is that many feminist scholars concentrated on creating conditions which would free women of their domestic roles so that they might compete more equitably with men in other arenas.

The paucity of research on parenting and adult development has been most unfortunate. It has helped obscure the tremendous potential for growth that the parenting role can offer an adult who makes a serious commitment to it. It has contributed to the devaluation of parenting, and to the underestimation of the enormous amount of work and skill involved in raising children and maintaining family life. This has made what already is an extremely difficult and challenging job all the more difficult.

Society has placed a higher value on activities that traditionally have been men's (i.e., marketplace work), and a lower value on activities that traditionally have been women's (i.e., family work). Greater power and status are acquired in the world of work than in the world of family. In an attempt to achieve equality, many women have moved out of primary family roles into the marketplace. There has not been a marked movement of men in the opposite direction. This can be understood partially as a function of the low regard in which these roles have been held. Society is in danger of going from being functionally one-parent families to being functionally no-parent families.

Unfortunately, many people have not understood the essential nature and importance of work performed in the family. In her book *Toward A New Psychology Of*

Women (Boston: Beacon Press, 1976), Jean Baker Miller described the extremely valuable psychological qualities developed in individuals who have been tending to relationships. She and Carol Gilligan, author of *In A Different Voice* (Cambridge, MA: Harvard University Press, 1982), are pioneers in describing the ways individuals can grow and develop in the context of relationships throughout the life cycle. For a long time we have been aware that a child's bond with his parents motivates and directs the course of that child's development. We have been less conscious of the way in which a parent's relationship with his child can be a powerful prompter of the parent's own growth. I believe that the parent-child relationship offers an adult a particularly rich context for development for several reasons:

• The unique nature and potential strength of the emotional bond between parent and child;

• The type of tasks involved in parenting, including helping to guide the development of another human being in a comprehensive way; and

• The fact that the relationship endures over the life course as few others do.

In parenting, one is confronted with challenges in critical domains of human development; the bond a parent has with his child can be a powerful force in motivating the parent to face those challenges rather than to avoid them. As a parent addresses these challenges, he can become a richer, fuller human being.

The capabilities to empathize, nurture, and connect emotionally with others are thought of as innate abilities. In fact, however, they involve a range of feelings and skills that need to be learned and practiced. Parenting certainly provides an ideal environment in which to develop or expand these abilities.

In trying to learn more about this subject, I reviewed the literature and talked with mothers whose current primary role is that of parenting. I will summarize briefly some of what I'm learning.

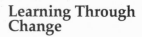

Seeing What Is Important

Parents who feel they have changed as a result of parenting often report an increase in self-knowledge. They say they have developed a clearer sense of themselves through their relationships with their children. They often say that being a parent has given them a better sense of what is important in life. This makes it easier for them to put life's events in better perspective; it can result in a change of priorities. Some parents describe an expanding sense of self as the activities in which they engage on behalf of their children enlarge their own repertoire of behavior.

Becoming a parent also can be pivotal in changing one's perception of one's own parents; it often leads to an improved relationship with them. Also, it can lead to the establishment of new bonds and ties with other extended family members.

Learning Through Change

In their book *Women's Ways Of Knowing: The Development Of The Mind* (New York: Basic Books, 1986), Mary Field Belenky and other psychologists report that most of the women in their study who were mothers named childbearing and child-rearing as their most powerful learning experiences. These researchers found that although parents acquire much knowledge on the job, it is the type of knowledge that is difficult to translate into words. It is also the type of knowledge that doesn't lead to the establishment of general propositions; this is because good parenting requires constant adaptation to changing situations and because it is attuned to the concrete and particular.

These psychologists state that mothers realize that what works with a particular child at a particular moment may not work with a different child or even the same child at a different moment. They, along with philosopher Sara Ruddick and Dr. Jean Baker Miller, say that mothers expect change and that change requires a type of learning in which what one learns cannot be applied exactly or even analogously to a new situation. In this way, they note, the type of thinking in which parents often engage differs from scientific thinking and learning; in the latter, an experiment is considered real or factual only if it can be replicated. This parental mode of thinking and knowledge is, however, no less valid or real than the other.

A parent accumulates a vast and valuable experience in dealing with change. This experience is one of the great challenges of parenting. It can result in growing competency in dealing with change. It certainly encourages the development of independent thinking and creativity. Miller stresses the importance of this ability to learn for change rather than fixity; she feels it is crucial that individuals in our society have this capacity.

Understanding Human Nature

Although it is difficult for parents to translate what they are learning into words, I believe it is important that they continue to try to do so, in order that they help us become more conscious of the extensive, vital knowledge the parenting experience can provide. Mothers with whom I've spoken talked about the difference between their previous intellectual knowledge of child development and their current, more profound understanding of this process. Their newer comprehension is based on their having taken part in the drama of another individual's development from birth onward. They feel that their firsthand experiences have made them more tolerant of different temperaments and learning styles.

They believe these experiences have increased their abilities to accept differences; they try to work within a framework of differences rather than simply try to get another person to change. They continue to try to influence others, but in a way that is more creative, more respectful of differences, and more appreciative of a person's need for autonomy. Dealing with their own children whose styles might differ greatly from their own has helped them broaden their understanding of human nature and methods of dealing with human beings. In general, they feel that parenting has helped them become more tolerant and less judgmental.

Acting As Social Agents

Lydia O'Donnell, Ed.D., and Marjorie DeVault, Ph.D., both have undertaken studies which help show aspects of the parenting role that enable adults to develop a variety of skills. In her book, *Unheralded Majority: Contemporary Women As Mothers* (Lexington, MA: Lexington Books, 1984), Dr. O'Donnell identifies and describes mothers' roles as social agents. By the term "social agent," she refers to the work that mothers traditionally have done to connect their children and spouses to the world beyond the nuclear family.

In their roles as social agents, mothers are the kin-keepers of their extended families; they establish links between their neighbors and their own families; they

learn about and select community-based activities for their families; they mediate between their children and child-serving institutions such as schools and physicians; and they establish programs and work in their communities. Parents often say that when their children were born, they felt a heightened desire to make the world a safer and better place; they actively work in organizations to help achieve these humanitarian ends.

Coordinating Activities

In her dissertations at Northwestern University, Dr. Marjorie DeVault applied a sociological analysis to housework. She detailed the planning, scheduling, monitoring, and arranging of housework which women traditionally have done and which is fundamental to life in the household. She found that because this essential, coordinative work cannot actually be seen, it often is unrecognized, even by those who are doing it. She defines this coordinative work as including both the physical job of maintenance and the work aimed at producing a certain social order, organization, and lifestyle.

Most previous analyses of housework have looked only at the actual tasks such as meal preparation and laundry. The planning, scheduling, monitoring, and arranging of housework have not received adequate attention. Dr. DeVault points out how dramatically this aspect of housework helps shape family relations and how these everyday activities can influence the overall character of family life. In the process of performing this role and in the role of social agent, an individual clearly is expanding her useful skills.

Parenting And Growing

Dynamic, active involvement in parenting can help adults develop valuable characteristics which not only would be useful in other spheres of life, but which also may be necessary characteristics if humans are to survive as a species. Clearly not all parents are able to use the parenting experience in this way. In addition, parenting certainly is not the only way to obtain these characteristics. Nor do I think parenting should be undertaken as a means of accomplishing these goals. I do suggest, however, that once an adult becomes a parent, the role can offer a uniquely rich opportunity for growth to a person who makes a serious commitment to it.

I hope that parents will reflect on the way in which they are growing while they tend to their children's constantly changing developmental needs. Parents should be aware of how they and their children are evolving in tandem, supporting and challenging each other to develop in more complex ways.♥ © 1987

Karolynn F. Coleman is the mother of two children, Gabrielle (fifteen) and Keith (eleven), and lives in Weston, Massachusetts. She is a clinical social worker and works parttime doing counseling, parent education, and research on parenting.

Becoming A Mother – A Journal

by Heidi L. Brennan

What does it mean to become a mother? For me it was the total transformation of my focus and even self-image as I assumed the responsibility and commitment of raising our child. The following excerpts from my journal capture for me the new feelings and shifts of expectations which came with my first pregnancy and the birth of our son.

August 28, 1983. John and I have been hoping that I'll get pregnant soon. I wish I wasn't so preoccupied with the problems at work. I would like to be able to pay more attention to my feelings and body at this time. I did have a powerful feeling on Wednesday morning that I could be pregnant. I am curious as to whether or not my intuition was accurate.

October 9, 1983. I am pregnant! My intuition was right. I can't believe how lucky we were. I feel almost guilty that it happened so fast for us while we have friends who are struggling to conceive. It almost intensifies my pain for them. Although I am excited and happy, I also feel ambivalent. Except for a little nausea, I don't feel or look pregnant. I just look like I've gained five pounds. I am irrationally scared that I will become fat forever. I worked so hard for so long to lose the weight I've carried around for years that now I am sad to be gaining. I know this will change when I can feel the baby and see that I am pregnant.

January 9, 1984. I feel fortunate that things have gone well with my pregnancy so far. Daily I think of various things I want to be doing as a parent, even though the opportunity may be years away. I spend a lot of time recalling my own childhood.

Now as I look forward to motherhood, I am in awe of the lack of maturity and perspective that I have as I compare myself to people I know who are parents. I have a sense of humility that causes me to laugh at my naiveté and say to myself, "Baby, you have no idea what it will be like."

March 12, 1984. At the moment, I feel immobilized with internal conflict. Will the reality of motherhood have anything in common with my current expectations? I am questioning my assumptions about combining childrearing with another career, even parttime. I think I am cleaning out my mental closet of beliefs about what I will be able to do and what I actually want to do after our baby arrives, especially when I talk to other new mothers and see how they spend their days.

April 9, 1984. Today is my thirty-first birthday, and all my thoughts and feelings are centered on impending motherhood. If I could have anything I wanted today, it would be to spend the day with my mother in California, as if to relive the meaning of birthdays in my childhood.

Well, that is certainly something I can give our child – that special, warm feeling that a birthday means – you are loved and wanted.

May 21, 1984. Charles Harry Brennan was born on May 19! What an unbelieveable moment! It is so difficult to describe the sight of a baby suddenly coming out of you to join you in your world. Being face-to-face with your child is incredible. In the hours since, I feel overstimulated – constantly excited, euphoric, amazed, and exhausted all at once. I have lost all sense of time. I am not aware of day or night. It feels as though it has been one continuous day since Charlie was born. I don't think it has even sunk in – impossible to absorb.

May 22, 1984. Even though I feel completely awkward at newborn care, from breastfeeding to diaper-changing, I do feel calm. It's my usual "even if I don't know what I am doing, proceed and assume that I do" attitude. It always helps when I am faced with uncertainty.

It is extremely rewarding to hold Charlie, to stroke him when he cries, and have him become calm. I feel an incredibly strong instinct to protect him. I am almost suspicious of the nurses.

June 1, 1984. Today was the last day of my mother's visit with us. It has been such a comfort having her here. I cried when she left. It is very hard to describe the needs and feelings one has for one's mother at this time. I think it relates to the feeling of having joined the club of motherhood, in which you are suddenly "in the know."

July 7, 1984. Charlie is seven weeks old today and growing fast. John and I are having fun with him as he shows great interest in his surroundings. Although I feel more capable and in control of myself than I did a month ago, I am still amazed at how time-consuming being the mother of an infant is. Things like going to the bathroom and brushing my teeth are accomplishments. A shower is a luxury.

August 24, 1984. I feel so much better and at ease as a mother. I think I have crossed some bridge to an area within myself where I am comfortable with the time demands and constant physical needs of Charlie. I am accepting the role of fulltime mother. I have to laugh at myself: even though school is several years away for Charlie, I read with great interest the local news on school issues.

September 8, 1984. I realized the other night that one of the unique and difficult things about being a mother is that one is such a beginner for a long, long time. I feel both respect and envy for experienced parents. I respect their competence and ability to cope and envy their seeming self-assuredness.

November 15, 1984. This is motherhood at its best so far. Charlie is just about six months old and is more wonderful than I could ever have imagined. All the books I have read say this is the stage where you can't wait till you have another. I have the same feeling. I'd like ten just like him. I have started Charlie on some cereal. Even though I plan to continue breastfeeding, I feel sad that this part of our relationship is changing. When he was two months old, and nursing for what seemed like fourteen hours a day, I couldn't wait to get to this stage.

December 24, 1984. What a wonderful feeling to be a family. John and I seem much more at ease as parents. Thinking of myself as a mother is no longer strange. Christmas is special to me this year in a way that it hasn't been for years. I think that the commitment and love which grow with your child exemplify the spirit of this season. I have never been happier.

February 17, 1985. This evening Charlie crawled up the stairs for the first time with John and me hovering over him. I sense a change in our relationship. He doesn't need me in quite the same ways any more and we both know it. I realize I must remember that his needs will continue to change and as a result, I will have to be sensitive and flexible so I can change with him. Allowing him to grow means I will have to grow, too.

What is sometimes frightening to me is that it is easy to wake up in the morning and just "be mother" – feed him, comfort him, diaper him. What takes more commitment and energy is to be aware of the subtle changes that occur every day.

Looking back over what I've written, I'm tempted to ask other mothers, "Do you think like this, too?" And yet, so much of our conversation is about teething, eating, bowel movements, sleeping, safety, and clothing sales. Why is it so hard to talk about becoming a mother? Maybe because even though it is a global experience, it is also intensely personal and private.

Charlie's first birthday is just three months away. In addition to planning a birthday party, I think I'd like it to be an anniversary celebration for John and me – to recognize our growth as parents.♥ © 1985

Heidi Brennan, Arlington, Virginia, is the mother of four children, ages seven years to seven months. Heidi is Co-Director of **Mothers At Home,** *the publishers of* **Welcome Home,** *and she is the author of "Transitions" in this book.*

I Will Remember Us

by Lori L. Dolezal

It is some time in the deepest, sleepiest hour of night. I yank myself from shadowy dreams and patter over the hardwood floor to your crib.

There you cry fitfully, rubbing your little nose into the mattress as you turn your head from side to side.

We are awake, you and I. We sink into bed – babe and breast connecting in the darkness. Hungrily you pull milk from me – the soft, silky nourishment that is depleting itself.

Your warm, chubby hand pats my arm. It wraps around my finger and we sit, a statue of oneness. Connected.

Daddy's snoring breaks our quiet rhythm. You stiffen. Sucking stops; eyes open. Hallway light is sliding under and around the door, light that your eyes eagerly find.

Is it playtime? Your eyes check mine and I whisper, "Shhh."

"Da da da," you squeal with a naughty-boy grin.

A lungful of laughter graces the night – mine, then yours.

Your head meets my shoulder, and we sway back and forth. I run my lips over your harvest of blond hair, then along your cheeks and nose, gathering all the warmth, softness, and innocence in my heart.

And with the unbearable pain of love, I accept the transcience of this moment along with the sweetness. I cannot forever be your source of life.

But when you are running full force into boyhood, farther away from me, I will remember us. Connected.♥ © 1989

Lori L. Dolezal lives in Appleton, Wisconsin. Her sons are ages seven, five, and four. She is attending night school once a week, working on her BA in English.

Child Of My Heart

by Mary Fisk Docksai

As I pause to light the four candles on my daughter Marian's birthday cake, my glance passes over each of the happy faces of the family and friends gathered to share the occasion. While we sing, and Marian makes wishes, blows out the candles, and opens the presents, my mind travels back to the many moments leading to this special day.

I go back mentally to Marian's third birthday, her second, her first; then further back still to her first word, first step, first laugh, and all the memories a mother keeps in the treasure chest of her heart.

I recall the first time I saw her. She was being carried off the plane at Washington, D.C.'s National Airport, by the adoption agency's volunteer – a tall, broad-shouldered, smiling military man returning home from Seoul. A flood of positive emotions washed over me: mostly joy, excitement, and relief that she finally was in my arms.

A few negative emotions surprised me by their presence as well. I questioned whether I could love her as much as I loved my son Rick, to whom I had given birth five years before. I felt some disappointment, too, that she was so big. The only photograph the agency had given

me showed a two-month-old baby girl. It was to this photo that I clung and spoke during the infinitely long four months we waited. The wait **should** have been less than two months. To say I was impatient during this time is an understatement. My frustration at the inexplicable delay was increased exponentially by the knowledge that with the passage of each day, her own adjustment would be that much more difficult. I went first to my Congressman and then to a Senator who finally uncovered the bureaucratic foul-up and facilitated her release.

My concern for possible trauma to her had been well-founded. At the airport, the lovely face of the six-month old baby who was to be mine was stormy, angry, fearful; those of the much younger children were not. The volunteer told me that she had cried most of the flight over, some twenty hours. She cried all the way home in the car until she fell asleep from exhaustion. I consoled her as best I could, and I feared for her well-being. Her wails went on for nine days and nights, then they stopped as she began to accept her new home.

The less-than-perfect homecoming was in some ways a reflection of the difficult path that lead to our decision to adopt a baby. Once we actually filed the first papers, we had to wait approximately eighteen months. We had to submit to physical examinations, scrutiny of our financial situation, interviews with our family and friends, investigation of our home and habits, and consideration

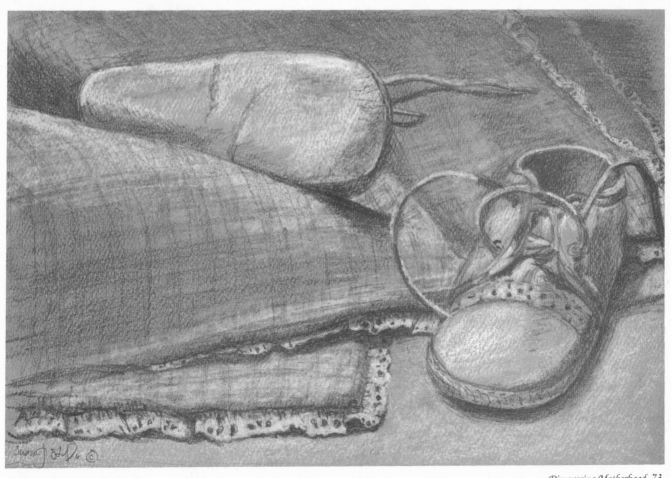

of our fitness to parent. I understood on the intellectual level that these precautions are excellent ones to protect the baby, but on the emotional level the feelings were of intrusion into our personal lives, resentment that we had to prove ourselves fit, and anxiety that somehow we would not pass muster.

My mind travels even further back – to the pain and humiliation of the infertility process, to the stress of trying to conceive, to the feelings of isolation and inadequacy that these experiences engendered.

I think it was the rigors of the medical experience – the attempts to isolate the causes of the infertility, the two operations, the waiting, the trying, the testing, and the reducing of the act of making love to a biological function on a par with ingestion and elimination – that eased the path to resolution of the emotional pain. Finally a sense of peace came with the decision to accept infertility and to adopt a child.

When I came to this realization I recalled an interview I had done some years earlier while working on an article about American couples who adopt children from other countries. I spoke with a couple who had adopted two children from Colombia. When I asked the father what it felt like to adopt, he thought for a moment, and then he replied: "It's like being given a precious seedling to nurture. Someone else has planted the seed – you did not. But you are to care for it, tend it, provide it with sunlight and nourishment and water, and all it needs to flourish – most of all love. And then you just stand back and watch it grow."

I thought at the time how very nice that sounded, like a saccharin greeting card, and how very second-best it must be to tend someone else's plant. Only time, need, and the kind of growth that comes through suffering allowed me to rise above this utter lack of appreciation of his powerful insights. The origin of the seed truly had become unimportant to me; like him, my need was not to plant but to nurture.

I reflect on how analogous the different kinds of pain that preceded the arrival of each child in my life are. With Marian it was the difficulties of infertility. With Rick it was ineffective labor, fetal distress, an emergency cesearean section, recovery from surgery, postpartum depression, and delayed bonding. While different, they are alike in one way that is most important: they no longer matter. They are only memories. Once I felt this pain, and it was significant enough that I remember it and probably always will; but the pain is long over and the joy is ongoing and increasing with each year. I would endure either again to have another child in my arms.

In some ways, it has been easier for me to mother this child than it was my son. Perhaps it was because he had come first, and I had much to learn. More secure and confident as a mother, I was more relaxed with Marian. Perhaps it is more, though. I now consciously live the words of the adoptive father I interviewed. I don't look for family traits: for Nana's nose or Aunt Kathy's eyes, or Great-Aunt Agnes' musical ability or Grandpa's sense of humor. (I don't worry about those family traits that should never see the light of day, either!) I don't know anything about Marian's genetic heritage, and I have come to like it that way. I just offer her opportunities, and as I watch her unfold, I take pride in her many wonderful aspects.

As I gaze at the faces of the loved ones who rejoice with me at Marian's fourth birthday celebration, I reflect on the ways in which the life of each person present is richer, fuller, and happier because of our birthday guest of honor. This is as it should be, for it is the nature of love to not rest content in itself but to splash over and water all it encounters. I begin to suspect that perhaps I have had it backwards all along. I had considered myself and my family as the gardeners nurturing the tender transplant. And so we have been. But while we have been busy tending her, we ourselves have been basking in her light and love. Almost without realizing it, we have blossomed as well.

My eyes finally come to a full stop upon the faces of Rick and Marian. His fair head is bent to be near her dark one; her brown eyes look up into his hazel ones. The wonder of their differences is yet another unexpected and joyous aspect of this mothering. I savor the strengths in him that are like my own; I savor the strengths in her that are not like my own. I enjoy in him what is like me; I enjoy in her what is not.

The doubt I harbored that first night at the airport has been long since laid to rest. I have come to see that in my well-tended garden is room for many wonderful flowers. My back is to the past and to the two different gates by which I entered, and my face is to the present and the future and the two young children entrusted to my care. And as I look at them, I am able to appreciate that gardeners can grow, too.♥ © *1991*

Mary Fisk Docksai is the mother of two children, the managing editor of **Welcome Home**, *and the author of "Chronicles Of Love" in this book.*

Resources

National Adoption Information Clearinghouse
Suite 1275, 1400 Eye Street, N.W.
Washington, D.C. 20005; (202-842-1919)

Bothun, Linda. *When Friends Ask About Adoption.*
Swan Publications, 1987.

Smith, Dorothy W. *Mothers And Their Adopted Children.*
Teresias Press, 1988.

Caplan, Lincoln. *An Open Adoption.*
Farrar, Strauss & Giroux, 1990

Melina, Lois Ruskai. *Raising Adopted Children.*
Harper & Row, 1989

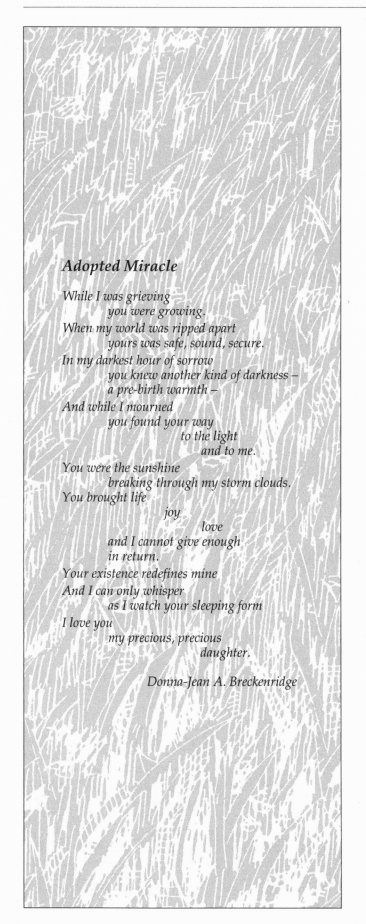

Adopted Miracle

While I was grieving
*   you were growing.*
When my world was ripped apart
*   yours was safe, sound, secure.*
In my darkest hour of sorrow
*   you knew another kind of darkness –*
*   a pre-birth warmth –*
And while I mourned
*   you found your way*
*   to the light*
*   and to me.*
You were the sunshine
*   breaking through my storm clouds.*
You brought life
*   joy*
*   love*
*   and I cannot give enough*
*   in return.*
Your existence redefines mine
And I can only whisper
*   as I watch your sleeping form*
I love you
*   my precious, precious*
*   daughter.*

Donna-Jean A. Breckenridge

Twenty Things
by Diane McClain Bengson

During a class on lifestyle, I was asked to list twenty things I like to do. I had no problem coming up with the twenty! Among them were reading, writing, being with my family, nursing babies, listening to music, cooking, hiking, and thirteen others. The next step in the class was to mark those items we had done during the last week, the last month, and the last year. The instructor's intention was to show us that we rarely made time for the things we really enjoyed; however, that wasn't true for me, a mother at home. In fact, during the last week I had done fourteen of these enjoyable things. During the last month, I had done all but two! The two I hadn't done? Swimming and counted cross-stitch. I do miss swimming, but the counted cross-stitch can wait! My hands are busy holding children now.

Perhaps the things on my list were rather mundane. I didn't list signing corporate contracts, snow skiing, or world traveling. And I left off things, such as seeing plays, spending hours browsing in libraries and bookstores, and taking reflective walks alone. But when I compare these things to hearing my sons' giggles when we play chase, being there to soothe hurt feelings and hurt knees, and holding small hands, I know these other things can wait.

So why did I choose to be a mom at home? Mainly, it is to be with my children. But it is also a lifestyle full of satisfaction – doing eighteen of the things I enjoy most!♥
© 1991

Diane McClain Bengson of Bellbrook, Ohio, is the mother of two children, ages three and eight. She also wrote "To Have And To Hold" and "Mothertime" in this book.

Down In The Cottonwoods

by Carol Pratt Bradley

When my grandmother returned to Texas after her honeymoon, my grandfather took her to live in an old adobe house that sat among big cottonwood trees. He worked in a dairy a long way off, and his day began at 1:30 in the morning. Grandmother was alone during the dark hours and many of the light ones.

Fifty years after my grandmother settled in the cottonwoods, I sat alone in our skinny townhouse; the baby was asleep. I sat in the total silence, felt it all around me, felt it inside me. The clock said 3:00 p.m. And it did not move.

I thought about Grandmother, and wondered if she ever had moments like this one in that first home. I wondered if the hours till her husband returned loomed long and lonely. I wondered how she felt and what she did about it.

They did not stay in that house long before Grandfather moved them closer to the dairy, and before my father joined them. I wonder if it was down in the cottonwoods or if it was later in life that Grandmother learned that there are cycles in our lives, a constant ebbing and flowing. Though life at times seems to be frozen forever into a single moment (3 p.m. for me), in reality time is very much moving and flowing under our feet.

Perhaps life is not a straight line, but a continuing circle, surrounded by the past and the future. We can lose perspective by viewing only the immediate. Such a view makes the difficult times more difficult; and when the sweet moments end, we think they are lost forever. Yet, they only have moved a notch in the circle and will come back around to us if we are patient.

To me, feeling isolated is to have lost my perspective. It is to feel my limitations, to feel compartmentalized, out of balance. We need balance to feel whole, complete.

To me a day that is whole is filled with variety. I can move through the day touching all the necessary parts; to hear silence as well as life-filled noise, to have the satisfaction of challenging mental work as well as physical, to feel the comfortable presence of others, and also to feel quiet contemplation.

To me, then, to feel isolated is to feel cut off from some needed part, some key ingredient to feeling life fully.

It is my own responsibility to discover and include what has been missing. Other factors may be involved, but I cannot wait for them to resolve themselves. I am ultimately responsible for myself.

Essential Ingredients

What are the ingredients that I want in that "whole" day? In my life, there are eight: music, books, have-tos, companionship, contemplation, talent-building, service, and nature.

Grandmother had no large stereo sitting in her front room, but I'll bet she sang. Did she discover the power that music has over the mind and the heart? When she felt lonely or sad, did she raise her voice and sing the sadness out of her, and sing in peace? I have.

I know that she had books. I have seen a notebook filled with her handwriting, in which she had copied down the words of great thinkers and made them her own. There always have been books to stir us, to share another's view of life through words so drenched with the richness that surrounds us that we can taste it, smell it, feel it.

There are always have-tos, those chores that must be done but do not seem pleasant or satisfying. For me, it is scrubbing the tile floor in the kitchen. Yet, after I make myself do it, that glow of accomplishment always comes, along with a feeling of freedom to move from the have-tos to the want-tos.

In that "whole" day, I strive for a balance between the comforting presence of others and the comfort found in contemplation. There is the need to feel undiluted love and caring coming from another person, and to be able to return it. That is why it is so refreshing to be with a child, to be the recipient of his spontaneous touch, of the warmth that radiates from his eyes. That is why it is essential to have honest friends to share ideas and feelings with, and to reap from.

The joy derived from others is enhanced by the contrast of being alone. The peace that can come with hearing the quietness outside the self and inside through contemplation is deep and strong. In my "whole" day, I need time to think of where I am, time to bring gratitude to the surface. I need time to dream of what I can become, for reality is always born of a dream.

Another important ingredient is developing some special talent. Everyone possesses some talent and a hunger to learn about and develop that seed within them – to nurture it, to share it. To do less is to waste.

Sharing ourselves with others renews and fulfills us. Self must be shared. We can develop the ability to perceive the needs in another heart, and the courage to act on those needs. Our capacity to give grows greater with every small act performed: we become a reservoir that fills itself. We leave the narrow tunnel of self for the broader, brighter view.

We are a part of that view, all that we see around us. Tunnel vision may prevent us from becoming alive to the sights and sounds and voices of our physical world. Our bodies are made of the same elements as the trees and grasses and animals. We must never allow narrowness to block off the feelings of kinship with nature. We can feel as strong as the mountains, as beautiful as the simplicity of a single flower, and as large as the sky.

In the winter the cottonwood trees around Grandmother's adobe house stood dead, white and bony. But inside the trees, the warm sap was flowing with the promise that it could come to life again and be able to give shade. Within us is that life-giving sap, a strength that courses through us, waiting to be tapped.

Perspectives

On the morning of their wedding day, before the evening ceremony, Grandmother and Grandfather took their first ride in an airplane – a two-cockpit open airplane with double wings. They paid for their tickets, stuffed themselves happily into the back cockpit behind the pilot, and saw the way the earth looks from the sky.

They saw the patchwork fields, the clustered towns, and the houses. Their vision expanded from the limited view down among the trees on the ground, to the freedom-giving perspective that encompasses all.

I wonder if Grandmother treasured that view in her memory, to pull out and remember when she was alone in that house down deep among the cottonwoods. Did she fly back up into the sky in her mind, see the way her home looked from that high view, see how it was a part of everything around it? And then did she feel a part of the whole?

Do I have that view?

And when she was up under that domed ceiling of blue – that sky that looks as though if you could reach up high enough, you could touch the hard edge of it – did she reach her hand up into that blueness? Did she see that, just as with the surface of water, her hand went right through, and there was no edge at all? No end? Did she feel that sky, and sense the limitless possibilities within herself?

Can I?♥ *© 1990*

Carol Pratt Bradley lives in Utah with her husband, her daughters Kristina (nine) and Shannon (four), and newborn Daniel. A former senior editor of **Welcome Home,** *she writes short stories and essays for publication.*

Time Capsules

Like those Russian dolls
within a doll,
all the you's exist
inside of me:
>*the small curled baby*
>*with chocolate eyes,*
>*the running toddler*
>*stuffed with giggles,*
>*the little girl*
>*who loved the face*
>*off Anna-doll.*

And though you stand
to my head now,
your legs fawn long,
your mouth too full
of teeth and spaces,
still, in the albums
of my head,
you run small again,
time lapsed and
fast forwarded,
and all the me's
that sleep in you
have faces like tintypes
developed in sun.

Barbara Crooker

What About You?

by Cornelia Odom

"I don't know how you can stay at home all day!" exclaimed my new acquaintance, disconcerted by the news that I am a mother at home. "What about YOU? Don't you want to do anything for yourself?"

It is not the first time I have encountered a question of this sort and been disconcerted myself by all of the negative things it implies about the decision to forgo, temporarily or entirely, a career in order to take up a life at home with children. My new acquaintance was not merely inquiring after my hobbies. Her question, asked without rancor, reflected the underlying ambivalence that many women today have come to feel toward the prospect of raising a family, an ambivalence rooted in a fearful misunderstanding of what goes on at home.

There is fear that being at home means literally that – being at home, all the time! There is the worry that in staying home a mother may fail to develop her abilities and may even negate her own inner life. There is the doubt that being a mother makes, in itself, any sort of real contribution. Time at home is time out.

How often do we hear of someone "taking time off" to have a baby or raise a family? No wonder women are getting the impression that time spent at home is time that really doesn't count! No wonder I am so unnerved by my friend's disturbing question, "What about YOU?"

What about me? I am certain there is not a mother alive today who has not asked herself that question. The greatest challenge of my past six years – and the greatest tension, too – has come from the struggle to give my two children everything I can while keeping something of myself alive at the same time. Like other mothers I know, I've been determined to keep some time set apart for myself, and I've used "my time" to pursue various goals and self-improvement programs. I've taken up hobbies and volunteer work, exercise programs and diets, continuing education courses and periods of self-directed study. But I'm beginning to understand that even worthwhile and enjoyable activities such as these do not begin to make an honest reply to that disconcerting question: "What about YOU?"

I am finding that I simply can't respond to that question with a litany of those accomplishments which are uniquely mine and which have nothing to do with my husband and children. I'm realizing that being at home, nurturing my children, creating the environment in which we live, being fully present in our home, *is* what I do for myself. That is to say, the life of the home nurtures me, too, and helps shape me into the sort of person I've chosen to try to become. An old proverb says it best: She who waters others waters herself.

I've never been able to balance the equation that would enable me to proclaim that staying home is my "career." Children are not production units, childrearing is not time on task, and my home is so much more than a worksite. But motherhood is certainly a vocation, a calling.

Our children's very presence in the world calls us, even in our sleep, even when we are away from them. Most new mothers recognize the degree of awareness formerly unknown to them. Even through the haze of utter fatigue is the light sleep that listens for the newborn's cry, the knowing that the baby is wet but not hungry, or frightened but not ill. As children grow older and begin to suffer their share of childhood slights and injuries, we know whether it is their body or their spirit which is hurting more. We know not because of the books we have read or the classes we have taken, but because we are their mothers.

Motherhood is a calling, and what it gently calls forth from any mother who will answer is a depth of experience and a quiet maturity that more than equals anything acquired in the workplace. Raising children is not an evasion of the realities of the adult world; neither is it an indulgent exercise in ego gratification. But it can be a sure avenue for personal growth and development, a spiritual discipline of a unique kind.

Motherhood is unique as a spiritual discipline because its practice requires neither ascetic withdrawal nor contemplative silence nor the acquisition of esoteric knowledge. You cannot mother from afar, only from the very center of daily life. It is the little choices that I make everyday as I practice my mothering, to be harsh or kind, giving or withholding, critical or affirming, which shape me and define me more clearly than any degree program or professional affiliation.

Mothering children calls forth a degree of selflessness and an ability to empathize that is hard to imagine coming by in any other way. Every mother knows that there are times when she has to put her own activities aside temporarily and attend to the needs of her child. When I was brand-new at being a mother there were times when I found it almost unbearably irritating to have to do this. I found it unbelievable that my day could be interrupted so many times and in so many ways by such a small child! It was only through being at home, by having to practice deferring to another out of love on a daily basis, that I have come to be less afraid of giving and more assured that when we act in love there really is, eventually, enough: enough energy, enough strength, enough time to go around.

Raising children calls forth creative energy we may not have suspected we had. It seems natural and good that a mother (who, after all, was for nine months an active agent in the very creation of her child), should be involved in the creation of his environment as well and in the shaping of his days. The hardest task that many new mothers face is that of bringing shape and meaning to their day. At home there is no pattern, no schedule, no goal, until you make one. When my first child was an infant I had days when I was virtually paralyzed with indecision. What should we do today? Should we go somewhere or stay at home? Or invite someone over?

What should we have for lunch? Should I try to finish all of the laundry today or attend to something else? What difference did it make? Having to constantly face such lackluster yet pressing details is one reason women today cringe at the thought of long days at home. But I found that by working through this initial period of uncertainty, I eventually found a new confidence and a renewed enthusiasm for the special freedoms being at home offers.

Despite the media image of household drudgery, years spent at home are years of relative freedom. When I worked, I did not have the freedom to keep daily company with friends of my own choosing. I did not have the freedom to set my own pace or, usually, to develop my own methods of doing things. I did not have the free use of my own time as I have it now. Every year that I am home I find more exciting ways to use that time creatively, both for my own satisfaction and for the benefit of my household.

Although being a mother requires me to focus on the lives around me, I also am kept painfully aware of my own shortcomings: my lack of patience, my sharp tongue, my sheer ignorance. Observing my interactions with my children has shown me things about myself that even my best friend wouldn't tell me. As one of my friends remarked, "I didn't even know I **had** a temper until Jack was born!" As for me, I didn't know how overbearing I could sound until I heard my daughter repeating my words in my tone of voice to her younger brother. But now that I do know, I can begin to change.

I don't think I exaggerate this point: in giving ourselves over for a time to the mothering of children we allow ourselves to be changed in positive and definitive ways. Yes, of course there are other ways to pursue fulfillment and personal growth. Yet for the mother who will accept it, being at home to raise children offers a singular chance to achieve depth and complexity during what is, in our time, a relatively brief period of life. The daily life of the home offers opportunities to teach, create, reflect, encourage, love, grow. Every day brings a new exercise in self-control, concern for others, maintaining a vision for the future. We work to teach these things to our children, but they teach them to us, too. In the end, what more could we do for ourselves than to take full advantage of this special time?

Being at home certainly will change you, but it need not diminish you. It is as much about receiving as it is about giving, and the self you find at home may be a gift that cannot be purchased with the remunerations of the workplace. So I have to reply to those who are concerned for my well-being at home that what I am doing now – for myself – is raising a family.

What about you? ♥ © *1990*

Cornelia Odom is the mother of two children, ages eight and six. She lives in Washington, D.C. She also wrote "Resisting Peer Pressure: Not Just For Kids," in this book.

About Our Artist

Susan Somerfield Stoffle, her husband and two children (ages twelve and eleven) live in the mountains of East Tennessee. They live simply, doing without a television, credit cards, and even a telephone. A mother at home, Susan has a home-based art business. She offers fine art as well as illustrations; she works in pencil, pen and ink, watercolor, and pastels. She writes, "Through a delicate and sensitive touch in my work, I hope to calm the viewers."

About Our Editors

Heidi Lawson Brennan grew up in Southern California. Her background and interests in communications, human resource development, education, and public policy have been valuable assets in her role as Co-Director of **Mothers At Home**. Heidi, her husband John, and children Charles (seven), Marianne (five), Caroline (two), and Daniel (seven months) live in Arlington, Virginia.

Pamela Makowski Goresh was born and raised in Pennsylvania. It was not until she started a family that she had the time to pursue her interest in writing. Her previous work experience in management and her years as a freelance writer, combined with ten years of at-home mothering, blend well in her role as Editor-In-Chief of *Welcome Home*. Pam lives in Ellicott City, Maryland, with her husband Andy and her daughters Samantha (ten) and Alexandra (seven).

Catherine Havrisko Myers is from New Jersey. Her first child was born in Mexico, giving her another perspective on cultural attitudes toward families. Cathy pursues her interest in self-directed learning and community development in her homeschooling family life as well as through her work as Co-Director of **Mothers At Home**. She enjoys learning about public policy issues and utilizing her publication production skills. Cathy lives with her husband Fred and children Scott (eleven) and Michelle (nine) in Falls Church, Virginia.

About Our Essayist

Robin Morris, whose essays begin each section of this book, is the mother of Richard (three). She is the author of *Welcome Home*'s "Perspectives" feature, and has completed the second draft of her first novel. Robin and her family recently moved from Maryland to Bloomington, Indiana.

About Our Poets

Marcia Crosbie, "(My First) Mother's Day" (page 4), and "6-13-89" (page 39). *Marcia is a mother at home near Lexington, Virginia. She is the mother of Joseph (three) and Forest (two months).*

Nedda Davis, "Multiple Me" (page 6). *Nedda is the mother of Ned (twenty), Neva (eighteen), and Nanda (five) in Reston, Virginia. She is working on a forthcoming biography set in the French Revolutionary period. Nedda was the poetry editor of* Welcome Home *for five-and-a-half years.*

Wendy McVicker, "On Leavetaking" (page 9). *Wendy writes from Athens, Ohio, where she lives with her husband John and their two sons, Leo (ten) and Daniel (eight). In addition to writing poetry and raising children, she is active in the Athens Friends Meeting (Quaker) and is a creative writing and library volunteer at her children's school.*

Barbara Crooker, "Perspective" (page 19), and "Time Capsules" (page 77). *Barbara is the mother of three children: Stacey (twenty), Rebecca (thirteen), and David (seven). She has had over four hundred poems published in a variety of magazines and books. She enjoys gardening and baking ("anything chocolate"). "Time Capsules" was first published in* Blue Unicorn.

Penny Snyder, "Jason's Trail" (page 21). *Penny is a mother at home and a freelance writer. She resides in Salem, Oregon, with her husband Buddy and their three children. She also wrote "Mouse Holes" in this book.*

Valerie Bryant, "Firstborn" (page 23). *Valerie is now a single mother, and a first grade teacher as well as freelance writer. Her children, Ben (fourteen), Kim (twelve) and Christen (nine) have won recognition for their art work and writing (short stories and poetry). They enjoy outdoor and church activities together in Knoxville, Tennessee.*

Beth Baruch Joselow, "2 a.m. Feeding For Thea" (page 32). *Beth is a poet and playwright. She lives in Washington, D.C., with her three children. Her most recent book of poems is* Broad Daylight, *published by Story Line Press.*

Jean Hegland, "Giving Our Daughter A Name" (page 33). *Jean writes and raises her children Hannah (four) and Tess (two) in the woods of Northern California. She is the author of* The Life Within: Celebration of Pregnancy, *published by Humana Press, 1991.*

Judith S. Offer, "Heather And Several Other People" (page 35). *Judith lives and writes in Oakland, California. She is the mother of two daughters, ages twelve and nineteen. She has completed two books of poetry,* The First Apples *and* Only The Words, *and she hopes to have a third book out this year.*

Cynthia Thomas, "For My Toddler" (page 38). *Cynthia lives in Waterville, Maine, with her children, Carrie (sixteen) and Heather (ten). Along with her poems, she enjoys writing in her journal on a regular basis.*

Alecia S. Lyons, "Family Arithmetic" (page 51). *Alecia is at home in Corpus Christi, Texas, with her children Jonathan (seven), David (five), and Rebecca (two). A former English teacher, she is now homeschooling her first grader and teaching occasional writers' classes and camps for upper elementary school students.*

Kristy Fickert, "A Mother's Prayer" (page 61). *Kristy enjoys country life in Springfield, Ohio, with her husband Chris and her children Lindsay (eleven) and Alex (four). She works as a social services consultant ten hours per month at a local nursing home and an adult day care center.*

Donna-Jean A. Breckinridge, "Adopted Miracle" (page 75). *Donna lives with her husband Bill and their six-year-old "miracle" Bethany, in Towaco, New Jersey. They are a homeschooling family, active in their church and are anticipating adopting another "miracle."*

Books We Recommend

by Lilli D. Hausenfluck

Seven years ago when I found out I was pregnant with my first child, I wanted to read every book I could find on babies, parenting, and mothering. I discovered then that writing about babies is a popular pastime! There are many more books from which to choose than a new or expectant mother has time to read. Reading ahead about pregnancy and parenting is fun and worthwhile. But the sheer volume can make finding a great starting point your biggest dilemma.

The following recommendations offer just that – a place to start. The fourteen women from the **Mothers At Home** and *Welcome Home* staffs who contributed suggestions have had thirty-four babies over the last twelve years! Undoubtedly we've neglected to mention many wonderful books, but we think these represent the best of the best.

I've organized our selections into six categories. The first five will supplement the on-the-job training your baby will be giving you. They are: Pregnancy and Childbirth, Breastfeeding, Child Care, Child Development, and Humor. Reading these books will give you plenty of insight as to the practical matters of child-rearing and will help you understand the unique needs of babies and young children.

The sixth category is different. Books in this grouping examine the indispensable role that mothers play in society. They help explain the nature of a mother's work and provide a solid rationale for the theme of this publication – that mothers who devote time at home to raising their children are making a great choice!

Pregnancy And Childbirth

These books give you a preview of what to expect when you are pregnant and alert you to issues to consider prior to labor and delivery. You will find information about your changing body, tips on diet and nutrition, and advice about what constitutes a healthy pregnancy and what necessitates a call to your physician. Many of these books end with advice on newborn and maternal health care for the six weeks or so following delivery. I recommend that you read this material ahead of time. I assumed that I would read it "when the time came," not realizing how exhausted I would be then!

What to Expect When You're Expecting by Arlene Eisenberg, Heidi Eisenberg Murkoff, and Sandee Eisenberg Hathaway, R.N. (Workman Publishing, 1984). See also their sequel, *What To Eat When You're Expecting*, (1986).

Guide To a Healthy Pregnancy by Donna and Rodger Ewy (Dutton, 1981).

Pregnancy, Birth and the Newborn Baby by the Boston Children's Medical Center (Delacorte, 1972).

Special Delivery by Rahima Baldwin (Celestial Arts, 1979).

Breastfeeding

"Although I was enthusiastic about nursing and I had great support from family, friends, and neighbors, it was more difficult in the first three months than I expected," reminisces Heidi Brennan, Co-Director of **Mothers At Home**. "After that, it is fabulous! You do need support. Find it; read about it."

We recommend that you read at least one of the following books before the baby arrives. You might even want to take one along to the hospital to refer to, along with the La Leche League International's new hotline number: 1-800-525-3243.

The Womanly Art of Breastfeeding by La Leche League International (Plume, 1987).

Nursing Your Baby by Karen Pryor (Harper and Row, 1973).

The Complete Book of Breastfeeding by Marvin S. Eiger and Sally W. Olds (Bantam, 1985).

Child Care

Books based on child care are like owner's manuals – they tell you what to expect from a properly functioning model and when to call for assistance. Some are very narrow in focus, other are encyclopedic. While their intention is to reassure you as to what is normal, *Welcome Home* staffer Nelia Odom warns that sometimes their generalized descriptions of pediatric ailments can be confusing and even alarming. When in doubt, don't hesitate to call your pediatrician or family physician. He or she expects questions from new parents.

There are many books in this category. Here are some which we consider to be modern-day classics:

Your Baby and Child From Birth to Age Five by Penelope Leach (Knopf, 1989).

Solve Your Child's Sleep Problems by Richard Ferber (Fireside, 1986).

Baby Sense by Frances Burck (St. Martin's Press, 1979).

The Fussy Baby by William Sears (Plume, 1987).

The Complete Book of Baby and Child Care by Benjamin Spock (Dutton, 1985).

Feed Me, I'm Yours by Vicki Lansky (Bantam, 1979).

Dr. Mom by Marianne Neifert (Putnam, 1986).

Child Development

There has been an explosion of research into child development issues in recent years, and it makes fascinating reading. These books help you think about what your baby may be sensing, feeling, and thinking. They also will give you insight as to how babies and young children learn and what you can do at each stage of their development to give them a rich and stimulating environment. It is important when reading these books not to compare your baby's skills too minutely with the descriptions of what children can do at each stage of development. Children are individuals and there is always a range for what is normal.

As you read about your child's developing abilities, **Mothers At Home** Co-Director Cathy Myers advises that you not feel too pressured by the emphasis, in the books and in our culture, on demanding early independence for your child. "Allow for some," she suggests, "but don't push and don't worry about it. Your child will teach himself to be independent in his own time. It varies from child to child by **years**."

The First Three Years Of Life by Burton White (Prentice Hall, 1985).

Babyhood by Penelope Leach (Knopf, 1983).

Infants and Mothers by T. Berry Brazelton (Delacorte Press, 1983).

Your Child's Self-Esteem by Dorothy Corkille Briggs (Doubleday, 1970).

The Magic Years by Selma Fraiberg (MacMillan, 1984).

The First Twelve Months of Life by Frank Caplan (Bantam, 1972).

Your One Year Old by Louise Bates Ames, et. al. (Delacorte Press, 1982).

Your Two Year Old by Louise Bates Ames, and Frances Ilg (Dell, 1976).

Humor

These books contain a lot of inside jokes, ones that you may relate to more readily once the baby arrives. They make fun reading on the occasional bleak days that all moms experience. They offer, in the words of Prudence Mackintosh, not advice but only "the solace of shared experiences." Whether you prefer Dave Barry's trade mark off-the-wall humor, Bob Greene's paternal musing, or Prudence Mackintosh's delightful sketches of life with three sons, it's always a pleasure to come across books like these!

Good Morning Merry Sunshine by Bob Greene (Penguin, 1985).

Babies and Other Hazards of Sex by Dave Barry (Rodale Press, 1984).

Thundering Sneakers by Prudence Mackintosh (Doubleday, 1981).

Mothering At Home

It's not uncommon for mothers to find that, although their hearts tell them plainly that their baby needs them at home, their relatives, friends, and former co-workers tell them differently. When those whose opinions we value are dubious, perhaps even incredulous, about our choice, it may not be long before self-doubt assails us. Is our education being wasted? Will we ever catch up in our careers? Do our children **really** need us? For mothers, these are the hard questions of our times. Fortunately, a number of excellent books tackle them head-on.

What's A Smart Woman Like You Doing At Home? by Linda Burton, Janet Dittmer, and Cheri Loveless (Acropolis Books, 1986).*

Sequencing by Arlene Rossen Cardozo (Collier/MacMillan, 1986).

The Heart Has Its Own Reasons by Mary Ann Cahill (La Leche League International, 1983).

A Mother's Work by Deborah Fallows (Houghton Mifflin, 1985).

As you can see, there are plenty of advice-givers out there for mothers and so much of it is truly helpful. In closing, however, let us leave you with one more piece of advice. "Books are great," says *Welcome Home* staffer Joyce McPherson, "but in the end you should do what works best for you and your baby, even if it contradicts the latest book!" What does Joyce, mother of two, do for *Welcome Home*? She's our Book Review Editor, of course!♥

Lilli D. Hausenfluck lives in Hanover County, Virginia, with her husband Bob and children Bobby (six) and Will (three). She serves as Chairman of the Board of Directors of **Mothers At Home** *and works part-time at home as a political and business management consultant.*

Lilli enjoys volunteering in Bobby's kindergarten class, playing racquetball, and reading spy novels.

*available from **Mothers At Home**.